inside/out

New writing from Goa

inside/out

New writing from Goa

Edited by
Helene Derkin Menezes & José Lourenço

[Handwritten inscription across page:]

For Shannon the best sister...

'Having a sister is like having a best friend you can't get rid of! You know whatever you do, they'll still be there!'

With love, Always

Amy L.

Goa 1556

Goa Writers

inside/out: New writing from Goa
Published in 2011 by Goa,1556 in association with Goa Writers.

784 Saligao, Bardez, Goa 403511
http://goa1556.goa-india.org | goa1556@gmail.com

Goa
Writers
http://groups.yahoo.com/group/goawriters

Goa,1556 is an alternative book publishing venture, named after the accidental arrival of Asia's first Gutenberg-type printing press in Goa in that year. It aims to create space primarily for non-fiction and fiction related to Goa. This project was undertaken as a team effort by Goa Writers and its volunteers.
Project management: Helene Derkin Menezes and José Lourenço
Design and layout: Aniruddha Sen Gupta
Cover photograph: Vivek Menezes
Typeset in 11/16pt Goudy Old Style by Aniruddha Sen Gupta
Printed by Rama Harmalkar (Ph 9326102225)
This book is partly funded under the 'Scheme to Provide Financial Assistance to Goan Authors' of the Department of Art & Culture, Government of Goa.

ISBN: 978-93-80739-11-3

for everyone who has a story to tell
and
for those who will listen

Contents

Introduction

What happens when a group of writers with a 'strong Goa-connection' decides to put pen to paper on a theme as abstract as 'Inside Out'?

Experiences emerge. Memoirs bubble forth. We try to make sense of what Goa means to us, within and without. If the collective past has shaped Goa, Goa now shapes us through daily engagement. We tell of how we perceive Goa, knowing well that Goa has shaped the very mind that now seeks to examine her.

If a Goan writer ever gets down to writing *the* story of Goa, that author can be assured of a chorus of naysayers who refute its authenticity and roll their eyes in righteous outrage until the tale accepts the status of being just *a* story of Goa – the *author's* story of Goa.

And thus the stories keep being told. Hundreds of stories, fables, novels, poems and scripts that conjure up shadows between the lines – elusive faeries that flit away when focused on.

In this maiden volume of the Goa Writers group, its intrepid members sally forth on a journey to the depths and heights of the Soul of Goa. Seen through the multi-hued lenses of these teachers, shopkeepers, cooks, flower sellers, engineers, tailors, journalists and other motley professionals, Goa rises like a spray of foam from the Mandovi, wetting and coaxing you, the reader on its bank, to plunge in.

And someday tell your own story of Goa.

Acknowledgements

To be creative is a gift but to have a mentor who encourages you and continually teaches you old things in a new way on your creative journey is a splendid thing. Goa Writers expresses profound thanks and gratitude to one of our most inspiring founder members – Victor Rangel-Ribeiro, author, musician, teacher and peacemaker.

Several workshops have been conducted since Goa Writers got together in 2005. We thank Victor Rangel-Ribeiro, Venita Coelho, Vishram Gupte, Himanshu Burte, Aniruddha Sen Gupta and Ben Antao for giving us their time, energy and creativity during these sessions.

The first meetings of the Goa Writers group took place on stools tucked between the bookshelves of Broadway Bookstore at Panjim, generously offered by its proprietor, Khalil Ahmed. Fundaçao Oriente hosted the workshop where we first met and also some of the subsequent sessions. The private studio of Mafalda Mimoso and the office of Vivek Menezes gave us an informal and yet intense ambience where we could rant, rave and scrutinise at leisure. Literati Bookshop at Calangute and the Museum of Christian Art at Old Goa also hosted our meetings. We also thank Dr. Délio de Mendonça and the Xavier Centre of Historical Research at Porvorim for providing an excellent atmosphere and support for many of our recent meets.

The locations for gatherings of the group held at our members' residences have ranged from Chorão to Carmona and from Aldona to Velim. Sucheta Potnis, Venita Coelho, Fatima Gracias, Wendell Rodricks, Helene Menezes, Prava Rai, José Lourenço, Savia Viegas, Kornelia Santoro, Aniruddha Sen Gupta, Amitav Ghosh have opened their homes (and kitchens) to host our hungry minds and we thank them for their hospitality. One memorable session even took place on a yacht – the lovely *Solita*.

One often takes online resources for granted, but we must thank Yahoogroups for hosting our virtual debates and interaction. Our group activities in cyberspace and 'realspace' were ably coordinated by our moderators Cecil Pinto, Frederick Noronha and José Lourenço. Special thanks to Cecil for coordinating our meetings, workshops and other informal activities that made being Goa Writers fun for all of us.

Margarita

Ben Antao

Velim-born and Margao-raised, Ben Antao believes that sex and money are drivers of human enterprise, themes that recur in his stories and novels, and in pursuit of which he escaped to Canada.

In April 1958 the stars began to shine on

Jovino Colaço with extra radiance – India lifted its economic embargo on Portuguese-ruled Goa. The border between Goa and India was once again opened, facilitating the movement of goods and people, and giving Jovino the opportunity for carrying out his smuggling operations via the rail route. In Goa, by and large, the people appeared content amidst the luxury of foreign goods. Most of the brash and bold nationalists were cooling their heels in jail, and those that remained kept their mouths shut in fear of reprisals.

The smuggling of imported watches and perfumes continued to feed Jovino's hedonistic appetite. And amazed at his own ability to turn anything he touched into profit, he began to ride on a wave of dizzying exhilaration as one whom the gods had blessed with all. That such a state of narcissism could prove fatal to a young police detective on the make hardly occurred to this galloping cowboy who, endowed with a first name meaning *jovial*, lived up to its promised legacy.

One sultry day in May he was coming into town, from Aquem to Margao, on his motorcycle. At the Saudades Road intersection, he slowed down, upon noticing a woman in the veranda of a house that had been kept closed for as long as he could remember. He grew curious, surprised to see an occupant there, and just as curious seemed the woman leaning on the railing of the veranda. She was staring at him as if she wanted something. He stopped his bike at the house fence.

'Hello?'

'Hello,' the woman answered, at once wearing a broad smile on her chubby face.

'I haven't seen anybody live in this house. You must be new here.'

'Yes,' she said, 'I arrived yesterday from Dar-es-Salaam, in Tanganyika.'

He remained silent, waiting for more information.

'With my children.'

Jovino knew that when Goans from East Africa came for a holiday, they usually stayed for a period of three to four months.

'On holiday?'

'No, to put my two sons in school.'

'I see. Well, if there's anything I can do, let me know.'

As he turned to leave, she said, 'Maybe you can help me. Please, come inside.'

Jovino hesitated for a moment; then, noticing her pleading eyes, switched off his motorcycle.

She led him into the sitting room. Must be in her late thirties, he guessed. She wore a dark blue, cotton skirt and a close-fitting white blouse that draped over her broad hips. He guessed her height to be around five foot five, and she walked with that easy grace that women seem to acquire after living abroad and upon becoming affluent.

'Please sit down, excuse the dust. I haven't had time to clean the house yet. What would you like to drink?'

Her query impressed and pleased him. She didn't ask whether or not he would care for a drink; she'd already assumed that. The invitation was music to his ears; and he was not about to turn down such a cosmopolitan gesture of good manners. He took off his pith helmet and set it on the flat cushion on the wicker-seat sofa. 'Scotch, if you have.'

'Please make yourself at home, I'll be right back.'

As she spun around, the heart-shaped locket on her gold-braided necklace bounced merrily, as if calling attention to the lustre of her curly shoulder-length hair. She passed through a half-opened door, poised and confident, with obvious knowledge of where she was headed and how to get what she wanted. She seemed so different to him from the likes of Maria Elena, the ones who made themselves important by patronising the lower classes and using them for their convenience. He liked confident women, of course, like Kamala, and already he was well disposed towards this woman. He liked her even more for saying, 'Make yourself at home.' He reached into his breast pocket and extracted a packet of Pall-Mall; as he finished lighting up his cigarette, she returned with a bottle of Black & White and a small glass.

'Please open it and help yourself.' She sat down in the wicker rocker across from him.

She used the word 'please' readily, he thought, a trait he found rather charming among Goans, another plus in her favour. But why had she not brought any soda or asked if he wanted some? Did she know instinctively that he preferred to drink neat? Goan men usually took their local *feni* neat. Perhaps she'd known that or had seen them do it. But foreign liquor! Maybe she had no time to buy any soda for she'd arrived only yesterday. He unscrewed the top and poured himself a shot.

'Cheers,' he said. 'My name is Jovino. I am a police detective.'

She looked bemused on hearing his title but refrained from commenting. 'I am Margarita. My husband is in Dar-es-Salaam. I've come with the boys. They are twins, both fifteen. They have gone out to look at the market. I want to put them in a boarding school. I'm told there's a good school in Monte de Guirim. Have you heard of it?'

She spoke with an urgency that he found rather attractive, contrary to the habit of local people who were disposed to be easygoing and relaxed about life.

'I know where it is,' he said and finished his drink.

She seemed glad to hear that, for finding a good school had exer-
cised her mind during her voyage from Dar-es-Salaam. Earlier at the
veranda, as soon as she'd made eye contact with him, she had sensed
that Jovino might be able to help her. She knew that in thirty seconds.
But, at this moment, she wasn't even remotely aware that she'd planted
a seed of desire in the fertile soil of his imagination. She studied him with
a slight tilt of her head. 'I hate to impose, but could you help me?'

Jovino watched her with more than normal interest, reading her
plea as an invitation brimming with possibilities. Thoughts of sex and
smuggling entered his mind. 'I'll do my best,' he said.

Margarita's tanned face relaxed in a flash, the tinge of anxiety
drained away from her soft skin as if her problem had been solved in that
very instant. She rocked several times, like a delighted baby in the swing,
her elbows on the arm rests, her fingers braided. 'Have some more.'

Jovino poured another shot in that easy manner of one who knows
he has earned his drink. He felt in control. 'And what are your plans after
that?'

She rocked again with a distinct suggestion that after her sons were
settled in school, she wouldn't have a care in the world. She'd be free to
do as she pleased. 'Then I'll go back. The school year begins in June, I
understand.'

Jovino was impressed again; she'd obviously done her homework
about boarding schools. 'You're right. And it gives us plenty of time.'

Sensing a rush of magnetism, he stood up and gulped down his
drink. Then placing the glass on the tray, he retrieved his helmet. She
extended her hand. 'Thank you,' she said, 'I'll pay your expenses.'

Her hand was soft but the mention of money lifted his already good
spirits. Still, he made it appear that money was unimportant to him.
'Don't worry about that. I have to run an errand in Mapusa anyway, and
I'll check out the school on my way.'

★ ★ ★

Januarius and Agostinho, the lanky twin sons of Margarita, seemed happy to be going to a boarding school in Monte de Guirim. It was the tenth of June, the first day of the monsoon season according to tradition. But there was no rain that day. Jovino, in a perverse, superstitious way, interpreted this non-event as a propitious sign. Having established the tenth of June as the commencement of the monsoon season, the local folks read any deviation as a good omen, depending, of course, on their individual objectives. Thus, farmers who had prepared their fields early and sown the rice seeds welcomed the rain if it came a day too soon, or prayed to the gods if it remained tardy. Jovino, keen to complete the trip to the boarding school without a hitch, felt that lack of rain was a portent his mission would be successful. He was seeing the rainbow before the rain.

The Vauxhall taxi and its driver waited for over an hour outside the white stucco school on top of the hill at Guirim, while Margarita inspected the facilities, attended to the details of registration, and settled her sons in their room. Around six o'clock, she and Jovino climbed into the back seat of the taxi. The car raced down the long narrow road cutting through the flat fields that were seeded and readied for the rain. Red dust swirled about until they reached the main asphalt road where the driver made a right turn. Other than the obvious sighs of relief exhaled by Margarita, the three remained silent until they reached Betim. Here the taxi adroitly rolled down the ramp and entered the ferryboat to Panjim.

'Oh, what a refreshing breeze!' said Margarita admiring the shimmering Mandovi River with the sun at her back. 'It was so hot in that school.'

'Yes, and humid too,' said Jovino, standing beside her at the railing and smoking. 'The rains should come any day now. The farmers are praying, no doubt.' He thought she might be amused by his comment but her expression did not change. Maybe she would welcome a cold drink.

'Would you like to have some refreshment in Panjim before going on to Margao?'

When she turned her face, a bead of perspiration glistened on her cheek. 'I'd rather go home. I'm tired.' Her brown eyes beheld his for a second as she said, 'I have refreshments at home.'

'Whatever you say,' he blew out a curl of smoke. 'I'm sure it will be more comfortable at your home.'

She turned again to face him. 'Jovino, thank you for all you've done. I appreciate it; I want you to know that. You're a sweet man.'

He smirked. 'Think nothing of it. I like to help people.' What Margarita didn't know, of course, was that he liked to help people only in ways to help himself. His help came with a price tag. It wasn't unconditional, certainly not a charity, and never a giveaway. He was imagining now how she would reward him. On hearing him Margarita's spirit surged with a rush of tenderness; she was opening up like a yellow bellflower in a garden under the gentle caress of the sun.

Although the route to Margao via Cortalim was shorter, this trip could sometimes be time consuming as another ferry had to be taken there to cross the Zuari River. The driver told Jovino he would go via Ponda and make it to Margao in less than an hour. When the taxi was passing through Old Goa, Jovino asked the driver to stop for a minute. He wanted Margarita to make note of some of the historic churches there.

'To your right is the Basilica of Bom Jesus,' he said. 'That's where the body of St. Francis Xavier is kept. To the left is the Church of St. Francis of Assisi, and further ahead is the Se Cathedral.'

At that hour this section of Old Goa, with its wide open spaces, radiated a rustic feel about it, with no traffic to speak of. The idyllic setting caressed with languid air uplifted Margarita's spirit. 'It's so peaceful here! The churches look so charming. I'd love to visit them one day.'

'Whenever you wish to come here, just let me know; I'll be glad to show you around,' he said with a gallant air. 'These churches have been here for centuries.'

'That's very kind of you; I'll think about it.' Her eyes now dwelled on a monument in the centre of the square. 'What's that?'

'That's the statue of Luis de Camões. He was a great Portuguese poet.' Like many Goans, Jovino had not had the benefit of education in the Portuguese *liceu*. He'd heard of the poet's name but had not read his poetry.

'Interesting,' she said.

The driver was smoking with his arm rested on the open window. On getting the nod from Jovino, he started the car. When he reached Ponda he turned off the ignition and said, 'Just one minute. Run out of cigarettes.'

They watched him as he walked up to the grocery store, a dozen or so steps above the street level.

'Let's stretch our legs,' Jovino said and got out of the car.

He looked towards the road leading to Manguesh and Mardol where temple dancers called *devadasis* lived. Ostensibly in the service of the gods and goddesses, the devadasis in temple culture often catered to the sexual needs of priests and other men. He thought of Kamala who was not a devadasi. He would visit her again one of these days.

'What are you thinking?' asked Margarita, seeing a playful smile on his lips.

'Oh, nothing,' he said, embarrassed to be caught thinking of sex. He was hungry and thirsty, and ready for refreshments.

The traffic being light at that hour, the driver made it to Margao by seven-thirty. When Margarita gave him a generous tip, the driver thanked her in Konkani, '*Dev borem corun tuca.*'

Margarita invited Jovino for a drink. While he remained standing in the sitting room, she walked into another room and quickly returned with a bottle of Scotch, a soda bottle and two glasses. 'Have a drink,' she said, 'I'll be right back.'

With his thumb Jovino pressed down the glass ball in the soda bottle. It fizzed delightedly, its sound caressing his ears sweetly, a soft lullaby that only a true drinker could appreciate. He was eager to slake his thirst after the long trip. He would relax, enjoy himself and take whatever she offered him. Margarita joined him after many minutes. She brought a plate of warm croquettes, sausages and slices of bread, which she set down on the teapoy. She'd changed into a loose paisley frock buttoned at the front, with the top and lower buttons undone. 'I find these soda bottles hard to open,' she said pouring the liquid in her glass.

'I know,' he said. 'Sometimes the bottle will explode if you're not careful.'

She raised her glass of plain soda and clinking to his said, 'I don't know how to thank you. I really appreciate the help you've given me this past month. Without you, I couldn't have coped. You've been a wonderful friend to me. I want you to know that.'

Hearing Margarita's fulsome praise, Jovino felt a rising in his pants. But he would be patient this time, wait for his moment. He poured another drink and as he was mixing it said, 'I love this whisky, it's so sensuous.'

'Taste the croquettes,' she said. 'I made them especially for you.'

So she had planned this after all. Appreciating her sentiment with conceit, he began the tease, 'And the sausage?'

She laughed like a flirt, obviously responding to his double entendre. 'That too, but I bought it in the market, already cooked.'

The rising was hardening as Jovino sampled a croquette. 'Hmmm. Delicious!'

She watched him like a woman who wants to please her man.

He fixed another drink, this time going easy on the soda. 'I'm glad things have worked out for you. Believe me, it was no sweat for me, I enjoyed doing whatever little I could.'

'Oh, don't be so modest. You've done a lot.'

Jovino felt she was stroking his ego beautifully. Cutting the sausage into two pieces, he lifted one-half with his fork and ate it ravenously, like a man being fed for a performance later. Then he took two quick sips, and polished off the other half. 'Aren't you eating anything? You must be hungry after the long trip.'

'I'll eat later,' she said raising her glass for a sip.

He was in the mood to play. He poked a croquette and extended it towards her mouth, 'Go ahead, take a bite.'

She hesitated briefly, then tenderly held his wrist and nipped at the delicacy.

Excited by her touch, he ate the other half. Having broken the ice now, he cut another sausage in two and forked a half to her. She clenched it between her teeth while he pulled the fork away.

'Have a sip of this,' he gave her his glass.

'It's been a long time since I had a drink of Scotch,' she said.

'This time is as good as any other.'

She sipped and gasped. 'It's strong,' she said stroking her throat with her manicured fingers.

'Drink some soda,' he said and she did.

A moment of silence ensued during which he sat wondering with his head bowed. 'How are you?' he asked her after a while.

She smiled at him. 'Good and you?'

'I am enjoying this, just what I needed.'

'Good, you're always welcome in my house.'

Jovino finished his drink and glanced at his watch. She watched him with a surprised look. 'You are not leaving, are you?'

'It's been a long day,' he said and stood up. 'I don't want to overstay my welcome. I don't want to impose.'

'Don't be silly, you're not imposing, not at all. Stay a while longer.' Then she advanced and kissed him on the mouth.

She smelled of crushed narcissus but her move did not surprise him. He returned her kiss with a long kiss of his own, a hungry kiss that searched her mouth as he tightened his hand around her waist. When he released her, she looked breathless, her eyes moist with heat. He kissed her again, now like a rooster digging its beak into the hen's nape. 'I want you.'

'Let's go to the bedroom,' she said.

In the small room the ceiling bulb was naked; she had the electricity connected just that previous week, she told him, and work on the fixtures was yet to be completed. She stood by the bed and undid the buttons of her frock. She wore no panties and the sight of her exposed triangle sent a thrill through him. He shed his pants and shirt in a hurry, pulled down his briefs, and kissed her with savage lust. Then he lowered her on the bed and she yielded to his rhythm. 'My lover,' she cried.

The next time he glanced at his watch it was midnight. She was asleep lying on her side with her frock barely covering her. He got up and dressed. Before turning off the light, he took a lingering look at her pubic triangle. In the sitting room he lifted the bottle to his mouth and took a deep swallow. 'Whoa!' he grunted in triumph.

Jovino closed the tall black wooden door quietly and stepped out. He walked to his place in Borda via the Saudades Road, feeling good and lucky that he'd played his cards right. In the Pajifond valley near the Hindu crematorium, he heard a dog bark and snarl at him, disturbing the stillness of the humid night. Turning his head to the right, he could discern in the distance, through a gate, the dog straining at its leash in the veranda of Police Chief Pacheco's house.

Photo by AGE (Gerry) Coutinho. From the collection of Carlos Coutinho.
A caminhão (old style bus) of Goa of the 1960s. Photo courtesy Frederick Noronha.

Walking as art

Isabel de Santa Rita Vas

Isabel tries to juggle many hats – the writer's, the theatre-person's, the teacher's being some of them. She is convinced she was born old and is growing younger – these things do happen sometimes.

Are you the lady who walks? –

demands the teller at the bank:
I've refused a proffered motor-cycle ride,
he declares.
I detect a twinkle in his eye,
Mercifully no resentment, just
a dose of tolerance for the eccentric
the silly, the impractical.
I laugh, no longer sheepish these days
About walking, walking.
Sure, everybody walks, some
all the way from the front door to the car.
Me, I walk past the car not waiting at the door or anywhere else,

Walk for the fun of it,
The adventure
The silence.
Not owning a form of private transport,
the alleged merits of walking could be termed,
who knows,
as a virtue out of necessity.

But walking can savour of poetry,
of contemplation,
to me, anyway.
I'm not sure if walking
Is poetry or prose
To the lady who sells fish at my door
Having walked decisively from Cortalim to Dona Paula.
Difficult to presume, one way or the other, these affairs
of prose and poetry
when you venture to walk in
someone else's *zotim*.
From where I stand
Walking as poverty
Is mystery
When one stops to consider

Questions of voluntariness
Matters of discovery in the involuntary too.
Walking as art?
It entices you with rhythm, colour, sound, texture, theme, beauty
Questing, condensing life.
Walking turns me out
Up and about
Inside out.
It strips me of protection and speed
It changes the pace of my life.

Walking reveals some of the dynamics of spaces
tight alleys where people stride with greater purpose and resolve
Wide squares
where folks assemble and amble

Public gardens
presided over by petrified freedom fighters
where the stray dog and the stray man
share the contents of a plastic bag
dripping curry rice and half a chapati.
And the *Sorticar* sits for a smoke
Wondering if if if the *sorte* he peddles down the city streets
Will ever hit the jackpot for himself:
Then he'd acquire himself a Bullet
or or or a crimson Santro
and
retire.

Children on the footpath, shouting, laughing like there's no tomorrow,
    redeeming.
Walking displays some signs of the times.
Traffic signals blinking, zebra crossings, harried feet,
Horns blow, swirls of dust settle on our eyelashes.
Youngster insanely mobile, on the mobile, multi-tasking.
Road rage.
(Hey, hey, hey, what'll you do when you get there – wherever – three
    whole minutes early, hanh?)
Signs of the times.
A shop named La Allegro next to another called Rash Deep –
- language and identity!
A stern warning at the entrance of a government office: NO SPITING.
A vegetable woman deftly balancing a heavy basket on her head, turns
    purple with fury and unloads the choicest, if not the chastest
    Konkani epithets against the chinky-eyed '*bhaillo*' vendor pushing
    a hand-cart piled high with tomatoes from Belgaum and oranges
    from Melbourne.

I remember the day I walked
a few miles
a few decades ago
one quiet early morning
when the Konkani/Marathi official language dispute turned crazy
and wiped all transport off every road.
My friend Benny arrived that morning from London-Bombay by the Bom-
      bay-Goa steamer. And of course he must be welcomed, agitation or
      no agitation.
The walk back home met with increasing fury
Burning tyres, bare-chested roughs gnashing large not-so-white teeth
blocking an undertaker's van
on its way to the morgue;
the van accompanied by a distraught husband, whose young wife had
      committed suicide – both long-lost classmates of mine, rediscov-
      ered in a chaotic world.

Walking often turns my eyes
this way and that and that
How else would I have ever discovered the double, concentric, rainbow
Perfectly ringing the sun? Ah yes, I stared for long, long minutes – and
      was indescribably grateful; and if you must know, damaged an eye.

Maybe there's something
About walking
That sets the creative juices flowing.
As with my play *Kator re Bhaji.*
The research had long been completed; writing the script was another
      ball game.
The proverbial agonies of writer's block! What form is the play to take?
It was on the road

That the bits and scraps took shape and meaning.
As I walk I meet faces
Some I've not met before
Many are people I know and cherish.
The enthusiastic wave
sends waves of cheer (and humour) into my step.
As when a one-time-student met me walking in town, tired after a long
    day's work and with big concern and small tact inquired why I was
    'looking destroyed-like'!
If you drive or ride
you'd never chance upon the guy I met yesterday:
You're Isabel Vas, aren't you?
Yes.
You teach at Dhempe College?
…Yes…
You do plays?
Yep.
You are from Aldona? You live at La Citadel Colony, Dona Paula?
Er… Do I know you?
No. But I keep track of people, don't I?
!!!
There you are. Easy. Walking makes you famous, maybe.

And walking gives me a lift.
Hey, can I offer you a lift?
The feet are consulted, they agree, it's been a long day. I hop in.
Time and time again,
I encounter generous souls
Who precipitously welcome me onto their bikes or into their cars.
Emmanuel.
Life is punctuated with lifts.

And often nuggets of conversation
that are gift and adventure.
I wonder, sometimes
How the motorist views the pedestrian.
Because the politics of walking
and not-walking
can't but hover in the polluted highway air.

My friend Solano tells me about his course-supervisor at Oxford, an 80
   plus genius of a green woman who cycles to work and refuses to
   patronise public transport.
To each her own.

Walking is my thing. I get to say hello – in homey Portuguese –
To every startled stray dog I meet on the way.
I walk to town, in my busy lovely town, in the still heartbreakingly beau-
   tiful villages – despite the ravages of the real estate catastrophe –
I walk, not invariably, but increasingly choose to.

I ponder:
Do I walk because I live in Goa?
Had I opted for Bombay or Hyderabad, would I have walked?
Had my family resolved, after 1961, to sail away to Lisbon, would I still
   have walked today? Had I chanced to be born in Nairobi or mi-
   grated to Sydney or São Paulo, how much walking would I have got
   done? Who can tell?
Questions of geography, economics, politics, culture, health … and art.
No regrets.
I unfurl my umbrella
in the driving evening rain
and since most other people have taken shelter

elsewhere
my hosannas rise along the road
dripping wet, off-key and loud.

Surprisingly,
I am surprised to find,
not other walkers, no,
but those who talk their walk.
In his thought-provoking little book, *Rain*, Sudeep Sen muses:

'I can walk anywhere from almost anywhere. I do not need timetables, or
ports of embarkation and disembarkation. I do not need guidance
of the tourist trade, or the help of someone who has done it before.
I just venture out; let my legs to the walking, my eyes do the seeing,
and my heart do the navigating. And amid all this, my mind keeps
me company, as I imagine, dream and see – visual and virtual, spon-
taneous and sure.'

Walking in company can be nice
But walking alone
Walking sort-of-alone-like
As the kids in my class might tellingly put it,
Is something else.
And does one really walk alone?

Encountering cyberspace: from the outside in

Frederick Noronha

Frederick Noronha's constantly changing facial hair grew grey in cyberspace. He has named his three children Riza, Aren and Goa 1556, the last of which has published more than 20 books so far. He sits cross-legged in cyberia like a venerable sage, promoting intellectual and internetual freedom.

Cyberspace can be one hell of a place. By
now, over a decade-and-half has passed since my involvement with the
internet. I can't help having mixed feelings about this period that has
been a crucial part of my life...

Because my low real-life profile is mismatched with my hyperactivity in cyberspace, some friends jokingly say that I only exist in cyberia.
The Net has made for me friends and enemies (a few, but angry ones),
brought feedback to my writing, earned me satisfying and meaningful
freelance work, allowed me to contribute to useful community causes,
and at times drawn intense bitterness from a few quarters too.

At the end of the day, are we insiders or outsiders in cyberspace?

Our generation cannot be called 'digital natives' by any stretch of
imagination. We are immigrants to this sphere. According to Wikipedia,
'A digital native is a person for whom digital technologies already existed
when they were born, and hence has grown up with digital technology
such as computers, the Internet, mobile phones and MP3s. A digital
immigrant is an individual who grew up without digital technology and
adopted it later.'

My first experience with computers was in my late twenties. After a
scholarship in (then) West Germany, I was toying with the idea of buying
an electronic typewriter. My brother, who had by then shifted from a
career in mechanical engineering to computers, pointed to a 'people's

computer' which a Government of India organisation was promising for 12,000 rupees. That AT&T computer never came through; but it made me think of the possibility of buying a second-hand PC and dot-matrix printer. 20,000 rupees was the bill – no hard disks, you saved on one 5-1/ 4 inch floppy disk and the software ran from another floppy!

It was in my thirties that I got a chance to use modems to transfer 'data' (at a crawling speed of 300 bits per second) from Goa to Bangalore. The newspaper for which I then worked, Deccan Herald, insisted we shift to transferring our stories by modem, even if it was then costly and painfully slow. Thank goodness for their insistence.

By 1995, I had gained access to the Net. This was due to an alternative network, working out of Colaba in Bombay and called IndiaLink (affiliated to the Association for Progressive Communications), that was providing connectivity to NGOs and journalists in those days. At that time even the concept of having a 'mailbox' in cyberspace, which one could access from anywhere, seemed a complex idea.

Hardly anyone else I knew was in cyberspace then. Most users came from academia or the affluent world. It was like talking to oneself. We did run into quite a number of expat Goans though.

But after years there, people suddenly began to notice the text and photographs I posted online. For a long time, it seemed as if these things didn't even exist. And when I had simply forgotten all about my posted content, inquiries started coming in. Sometimes the queries were strange. They could range from how best to sell paneer in Goa (from a vendor in Hyderabad) to how to find a life-partner through a cybermatrimonials column linked to Goa.

At other times, the postings in cyberspace brought in useful freelance work, always a boon to anyone trying to build independent and sustainable operations in the media. A plethora of story ideas kept coming in from cyberspace. At one stage, an editor and some colleagues found my emphasis on the outside world, and the fact that so many of my subjects were foreign, to be strange, if not suspicious. But then, the cyberworld has no borders. 'Inside' and 'out' are blurred, at best.

★ ★ ★

My own romance with cyberspace started without much warning, and is one that perhaps enfolds other stories within it. It was in 1993-94, just as I was venturing into freelancing, knowing that the Internet was slowly becoming a reality, while skeptical colleagues kept issuing dire warnings against making such a move.

In Goa, an email address was still an oddity then. My first experience with a modem came about (as mentioned, thanks to Deccan Herald) in 1990. One needed a license to operate a modem in those days. The irony was that even the seniormost officials of Goa Telecom (as it was then known) didn't know what a modem was, or how to issue a license! 'Something like a fax,' was how they viewed it!

Four years later, Prof Gurunandan Bhat, then at the Goa University (a Physics man who opted for Computers, and he was brilliant at both) was showing us one of the first Mosaic browsers. We didn't realise how new it all was then. But the Internet as we now know it was just taking shape. It was moving out of academia and defence initiatives and reaching the outside world. Webpages and tonnes of information were now becoming available to just about anyone, even those who didn't possess much technical skills to access it.

Spam and porn were hardly as ubiquitous as now.

I came to own my first modem sometime in the early nineties. It was a US Robotics modem, bought from my friend Joseph 'Boogie' Viegas, a tech-guru and early pioneer of cyberspace. Boogie and I had a very public spat ('People had warned me that you were a yellow journalist!') due to a misunderstanding in cyberspace but that's another story. He had then set up base on a still-green Alto Porvorim hillock. He has since moved on to greener pastures, in another sense, to Canada.

Modems were then costly, and the 14.4 kbps modem came at 14,000 rupees. But yes, the risk was well worth it ... even if it meant spending a large chunk of one's life savings then. I don't regret it, it was perhaps one of the best decisions I have ever taken.

You can now buy a modem that's nearly 18 times faster for barely one-tenth the price. But that early investment helped me to learn a new field, to expand my vistas and make freelancing viable. It even allowed me to engage in cyberspace at a time when everyone out there seemed far more helpful and far less cynical.

My first involvement with networks in cyberspace was via Goanet, which completed 16 years of meaningful, controversial and lively existence in August-September 2010.

Goanet (also spelt as GoaNet or even Goa-Net in those days) was, and is, largely an electronic mailing-list based operation. Its website is at www.goanet.org. A mailing list simply means one can send mail to a large number of people, and is a very inexpensive and powerful way of communicating. Of course, many people get put off by the fact that mailing-lists are almost always volunteer-driven initiatives, and it's hard to get paid for working on them.

I learnt of Goanet through Canada-based Tim de Mello. He explained how it worked via a letter-to-the-editor in the Ashwin Tombat-edited Gomantak Times, if I recall right. One thing led to the other... It was love at first sight with Goanet.

★ ★ ★

As a journalist, my first thought was about how this new medium could widen possibilities for expressing ourselves, and for free speech. Which journalist has not run into roadblocks that somehow prevent 'your story' from getting told? Whether blocked by a lack of space, an editorial decision, or whatever, this happens all the time. Earning was quite another issue; there didn't seem to be even remote possibilities for this at that time.

The dream started working. Maybe subconscious wishes get translated into action, in some deep, mysterious manner.

As mentioned earlier, I had just got access to the Net with help from IndiaLink, an NGO-backed initiative. To access cyberspace we had to dial up all the way to Mumbai and access our mailbox.

We usually did this once daily, after 10 pm, to benefit from the off-peak late-night rates. Fortunately, those were still pre-spam days. Yet, we kept fingers crossed each time we dialled out, hoping that not 'too many' messages would be awaiting us, clogging up our in-box.

I soon gained allies among the enthusiasts at the Herald International Review. Goldwyn Figueira, Agnelo Rodrigues and Susan Fernandes of the Review team agreed to officially share news from Goa out into cyberspace. Then, as now, most were suspicious about sharing 'for free'. Newspaper managements were approached by Eddie Fernandes, who later became a Goanet Volunteer and Admin Member. But they were thrown off balance by the lack of a logical 'revenue model' here.

Vishwas Chavan, then a young scientist at the Dona Paula-based National Institute of Oceanography, had already been sending out news to Goanet. He did so more as a volunteer than as a journalist, and his role was appreciated.

On joining, Goanet founder Herman Carneiro surprised us with a 'welcome to the list' message, that went out on-list. Everyone would get one of those 'welcome notes' those days, even if it was a cc (carbon copy) posted to all new members and the list. Numbers were still tiny, there must have been a hundred or less people reading Goanet in those days.

★ ★ ★

Eddie Fernandes, who currently runs the neatly-crafted Goanvoice.org.uk, was one of my first overseas contacts who got back in a detailed way. At that time, he was an engineering librarian at the University College London, a job from which he has since retired. Eddie was very helpful in sharing information and inputs.

In no time, he sent across an entire cassette tape — recorded with

a lengthy, but interesting monologue in his own voice. He chose this as
the medium to share his thoughts with me, instead of writing a long
letter! He also shared some 3.5 inch disks of news-clippings relating to
reports on Goa going back to the eighties, a valuable trove of information in those pre-Internet days.

Later entrants to cyberspace sometimes believe that there are vested
motives behind sharing. Taking part in the 'gift-economy' – where we
share our abundance, specially digital 'goods' which definitely don't get
depleted by sharing – benefits us all. And none of us become poorer for
it.

Without doubt, I personally gained hugely. Even by way of freelance assignments. But it would be untrue to say that I got involved in
cyber-sharing with some grand plan of benefitting out of it in a selfish
sense. Whether it yields returns or not, I would probably continue it in
one way or another. It does lend a whole new meaning to life.

★ ★ ★

Along the way, friends on Goanet decided I could do with a digital
camera. It then cost around two hundred dollars, and was one of the
early models - an Agfa e304.

It took pictures at an incredibly low resolution, but fine enough for
those days. Each photo-file was under 40 kilo bytes in size! Yet, this allowed me a head-start in sharing photographs online, and it also impressed the techno-savvy late Pramod Mahajan of BJP on a visit to Goa!
Today, I share over 30,000 high resolution photographs of Goa via
http://goaphotos.notlong.com, and feel I have more than paid back for
this early gift.

In this way, contacts were built, one by one. Every link was like a
giant step into cyberspace.

Friends like Ulysses 'Uly' Menezes created a neat and impressive
web-page with my photographs of Goa. Marlon Menezes, the man behind Goan-Web (the first web-site focussed on Goa), GoaCom.com (in

part) and GoaCom.org, was also supportive and we worked together for a long time, sharing news, tech skills and server space.

I subsequently became part of the Goanet-Admin team, helped send out 'news' from here, and also helped organise the annual Goanetters' December-end meets here in Goa.

But managing to do something positive in cyberspace always depended on having a suitable team. There were many. First of all Herman, Eddie and Marlon themselves, Bosco D'Mello, Vivian(a) Coelho, Sunila Muzawar, Avelino in the Gulf, Christina who looked after the CyberMatrimonials listings, Selma who did the summaries, and so many others. While we may have disagreed, or even shared hard words, it was a pleasure to get to know one another and work together.

★ ★ ★

In 2006, a dozen years after Goanet was born (and around eleven years after my involvement with it), a query raised by one reader made me think. He said something to the effect of – 'It's a fine job you guys (the Goanet admin team) are doing... but have you thought about who will follow in your footsteps once you guys are no longer there?'

Suddenly it struck me; there was an element of truth here. Life has to go on. Eleven years is a long time. It was time to move on. But de-addicting oneself from an interesting project like Goanet is not easy. I keep up my involvement there, but in varying ways.

Over the years, many different realities struck home. Cyberspace is a great place, but it is one full of egos too. Many people – especially in the earlier times – were very helpful, and eagerly wanting to 'give back'.

Unfortunately, as cyberia grew in stature and impact, it started attracting the wrong kind. Increasingly, those who came on board – a small number, but big enough to severely rock the boat – were there with a what's-in-it-for-me approach. Others would use cyberspace as a soapbox to boost their own ego, fight and abuse those they didn't agree with, and personalise debates in a big way.

At the same time, there is so much that is positive, still flowing out of cyberspace. Ideas of 'inside' and 'out' all depend on how we construct this space in our minds. Much of these divisions are man-made and artificially constructed.

It was young Herman's initiative that showed us the way. Without doubt, this experience helped up build other ventures in cyberspace. We – not just me but also friends who wanted to try our parallel experiments – applied the Goanet concept to start over half-a-dozen or so village-based Goa networks. There were many other networks, like the ones promoting Free Software to writers' discussions, and others working on greenery and Goa-Research-Net. BytesForAll was another such venture that was hugely successful at one point of time, and won an honorary mention in the Prix Ars Electronica contest in Austria in 2001.

★ ★ ★

Any regrets? A few. But let that not out-shadow the many things that went right.

Sometimes, one gets a bit upset by bitterness and backbiting, but then there is appreciation and kind words too. It is unfair to expect people to be eternally grateful for volunteer work, I realised. The reward comes from the satisfaction of knowing you've done a good job.

Criticism came from some quarters and left a bad taste in the mouth. But, in the writing world, one has to realise that people often criticise you just because their point of view (and bias) conflicts with yours. One way is to simply accept this. The tougher question is how to create more space to accommodate our king-size Goan egos!

My second regret is about the manner in which dreams get hijacked and taken over. When we criticised Goa, it was neither because of hatred for the place, nor a justification for leaving and migrating from this region. Over time, the criticism that tinted my reportage in cyberspace seems to have become useful cannon-fodder for people with various agendas. Like making a case of why Portuguese colonialism was really better, or critiquing a political party in Goa to subtly show that the 'alternative' (never mind that it's much of the same) is indeed superb.

Another regret is that Goanet today seems to be becoming a victim of its own success. Its free-speech policy means anything goes. With its membership growing (almost 14,000 across its diverse lists), more people are finding it a useful soap-box through which they can peddle their message.

It is a dilemma of how to ensure that 'editorial control' doesn't block the debate, while at the same time ensuring that quality and non-repetitive posts get preference. Of course the question that would always come up would be: who defines quality?

Despite all this, there are many reasons to be optimistic. I've learnt from cyberspace, and it has shaped my attitude and approach. It has taught me that sharing is power, and that knowledge should be shared equitably. To everyone that shared this journey, I owe a great and un-repayable debt. Cyberspace plays a big role today to complement and supplement what the mainstream media is doing back in Goa.... and to open up discussion space where it is lacking.

Moebius

Aniruddha Sen Gupta

Aniruddha Sen Gupta likes to laugh and make people laugh, but when he starts writing, some other personality emerges and takes over. He's had a couple of books published and that's gone to his head, so he's going with the flow.

Topping the rise, the old man paused to soak

in the beauty of the landscape before him. The road wound its way down the hill, seeming to find its own path like a stream of water. Surrounding it was a tapestry in shades of green, patched here and there by fields with laterite stone borders. In a small cluster, tall coconut trees stood like sentinels over a few houses – all with white walls and red-tile roofs.

He called out to his grandson, who had traipsed a little distance ahead, 'Slow down, Connie.'

The little boy turned and ran back up the hill to him. In his hand was a stick which had been transformed into a sword.

A man was wheeling his cycle up the slope. Coming abreast of them, he grinned, showing a periodically interrupted row of discoloured teeth, and greeted the old man, '*Deo boro dis dium*, Conrad-bab. Heading home?'

The sweet smell of cashew-fruit wafted out along with the words.

'*Deo kurpa dium*, Adozio,' he replied. 'Yes, as always.'

Adozio disappeared over the hill, and the two of them continued down the road. Little Connie was looking quizzically at his grandfather.

'Why do you have the same name as me, *xapai?*' he asked.

Conrad gave the question some thought, as he did all of the boy's questions, however innocent or innocuous. Everyone deserves a straight answer, he believed. So what if Connie was just a child? The truth was his birthright as well.

'Because everything repeats itself,' the old man finally said. 'Like the earth goes around and around, bringing day after night and night after day. Even life comes around like that.'

Now it was the boy's turn to give the idea some thought. He was a serious child, and given to grave contemplation of his experiences.

'Does that mean one day I will be you?' he asked.

'In a sense, yes. You will certainly be *like* me.'

He hoped he was correct. His dreams were invested in that direction. Ever since Connie had passed into his care, he had put all his effort into shaping the boy in his own image. The effort he ought to have expended on his own son, Connie's father, Carlos. He realised that now.

But at that time, when he was a young, brilliant physics scholar, with a comet-like future prophesied for him, his sights had been trained elsewhere. Pinpointed on that next rung of the academic ladder, the next path-breaking paper, the fiercely fought-for research grant, the chair at the famous university. His family had drifted on the edges of his consciousness, little more than bugs that only attracted his attention when they annoyed him.

As Carlos had grown older, started going to high school, he had gradually started coming into focus for Conrad, by then a professor of some renown. One evening, exhilarated by the insight shown by one of his more promising students in class that day, he had suddenly, at the dinner table, begun talking to Carlos about the structure of the universe. He marvelled at how going smaller and smaller – down to the microcosmic realm of the atom and its electrons – one reached a state which paralleled the structure of solar systems, galaxies, universes. He likened it to Babuskha dolls, universes within universes, within universes, ad infinitum.

He was so caught up in his own explorations, he hardly registered that Carlos was staring at him with a look of dumbfounded shock. He only saw it when he was brought back to the present, the life-sized, the real, the human, by Martha's irritated, 'Oh, Conrad, let the boy eat. He has a game tomorrow, and needs to sleep early.' It was a double jolt – one, to realise that Carlos had no idea what he was talking about and, two, to recognise that he had no idea that Carlos played some sport, let alone what game it was.

Over the next few weeks, he tried to get to know Carlos better. He attended the game – it was a school football match, and Carlos's team won. He asked him questions about his school life, his interests, his ambitions. But Carlos, unused to such paternal probing and made apprehensive by it, retained a taciturn opacity, and his father found himself feeling frustrated.

Conrad also tried to begin imparting to his son, as he had done at the dining table, his insights into the physical universe, his wonder at the complexities and intricacies of its discernible patterns. In this, more than the other, he hit a brick wall. After a few weeks, he was forced to accept that his son was blind to this vision of his.

Over time, Carlos had taken a path that led him out of his father's life. Traversing terrains that Conrad had no conception of, and could therefore provide no directions for, Carlos had wound up on a ship, doing little better than what Conrad saw as manual labour.

He knew that it could have been an innate inability on the part of his son that had closed Conrad's world to him, but he feared that it was instead his lack of involvement in the boy's life when the lad had been younger and more able to learn.

It was this guilty apprehension that had dictated his approach with his grandson. From the moment he could, he had begun to tell the young child of the things he knew, the secrets the universe had revealed to him, like an illusion only a few can see through. He had always been a good teacher, and he knew how to make a lesson sound like a fascinating story, and how to turn a boring activity into a fun game.

Now, as they neared the chapel, he walked over to the low wall where the two of them always took a break. He sat there and contemplated the rich green fields opposite. Connie was swishing his sword at some bushes nearby, decapitating a few small flowers.

'Come over here, Connie,' the old man said. 'Sit down for a little while.'

The boy came over, obedient as always, but with a quick slash at a protruding branch to express his independence.

'Give me your notebook, and I'll show you something interesting.'

The old man took the proffered notebook and, opening it to the blank last page, tore off a thin strip of paper all along the edge of the page, then another. Tucking one strip under his thigh to prevent it from flying off, he folded the other into a ring.

'Take your pen,' he told the boy, 'put it next to where I'm holding the paper with my thumb, and run it around the paper without stopping.'

Connie did so, completing a thin blue line that ran almost all the way around the ring.

Without letting it unfold, his grandfather slipped the ring of paper under his other thigh, and pulled out the blank strip. He folded this strip as well, but gave it a twist before joining the two ends.

'This, Connie, is called a Moebius strip,' he explained. 'It looks so much like the ring you just marked, but it's very different. Mark this one with your pen, like you did the other paper.'

Connie did as he was told. It was more difficult to complete this line than the other one had been. When the pen passed the joint, the boy found that he was drawing on the inside of the strip, and it took some bodily contortions on the part of grandfather and grandson to get the pen back to its starting point without lifting it off the paper's surface. When the boy was done, Conrad let go of the joint, and the paper ribbon fluttered in the wind, held only at one end. The old man fished out the paper he had stuffed under his thigh.

'Look at the two marks,' he told the boy. To Connie's wonder, the first strip was marked only on one side, but the Moebius paper had a blue line on either side of it.

'But I only made one line,' he said, his eyes widened and his voice hushed at the miracle.

'Yes, that's the amazing thing about the Moebius,' his grandfather replied. 'It looks like it should have two sides, but it has only one. Here, I'll show you.'

He refolded the strip and the boy studied the twisted ring that resulted.

'Some scientists believe that the universe itself is like a Moebius strip, which twists around on itself. Its inside is its outside, and its outside is its inside. And if you could travel across the entire universe, you would eventually be back where you started. Though,' and here he leaned toward the boy and looked comically menacing, 'you would be turned inside out.'

'No, I wouldn't, *xapai!*' the boy whispered, searching his face for a sign of jocularity, 'Would I?'

'No, Connie, the last bit was just a joke,' he laughed, and the boy joined in, still a little uncertain.

'Can I please have the inside-out strip, *xapai?*' the boy asked, as they got up to go. Conrad looked around, and spotted the plant he was searching for, the *chandado*. He broke off a twig and rubbed the two pieces together. Using his finger to scoop out the sticky sap that formed, he applied it to the two ends of the paper strip, gluing the Moebius into shape. He handed the strip to the boy, who played with it as he walked.

Conrad, whose career had ridden on his special gift for recognising patterns, ruminated on what he had just explained to his grandson. The words could so easily have been used to describe his own life. He was certainly back to where he had started, in the little Goan village where he had been born. But in some ways, he had indeed been turned inside out in the long journey between setting out and returning.

It had been a little over a year ago, and he had been on the verge of retirement. Far from home, in the city he had adopted, and which had adopted him. Waking up one morning to find Martha still in bed beside him, which was unusual for her. Trying to wake her up and gradually coming to the realisation that he never would be able to. The university had granted him his request of a slightly premature retirement on humanitarian grounds, and he had returned to his once and future home. Alone for the first time in his life.

Then, within four weeks of his return, had come the bigger blow. Bigger for being so unexpected, so unkind. A letter had arrived from Carlos's shipping company, informing 'whosoever may receive this' that there had been an accident. The ship had been transporting chemicals, and Carlos had gone down into one of its cavernous holds in a routine inspection.

He had not come back out. Not alive, at least.

The matter-of-fact letter was followed a week later by Carlos's wife, Anita, whom he hardly knew and their four-year-old son, Connie, whom he didn't know at all. They had till then been only two-dimensional beings from photographs that he had seen, and not cared to convert to flesh and bone. But it was with their coming that his own ghost of a life gradually gained a corporeal form.

The boy and the old man were now close to home.

Connie, skipping ahead, saw his mother standing on the balcao, and ran towards her, waving. Behind him, Conrad felt a sudden moment of disorientation. For a moment, it was Martha waiting for them, and Carlos was running back home. He shook his head to bring the present back into focus. Everything comes around, he thought, but sometimes things get turned inside out in the process.

Aniruddha Sen Gupta, 'Boats', Aldona, Goa, 2011

Bulletproof

Kornelia Santoro

'Everything is possible' – German writer Kornelia Santoro chose this
credo early on. After travelling through India on an Enfield Bullet, she
settled in Goa with her Italian husband and son.

'They put all the necessary pieces into a basket, you pay for the basket and after some days of work you have a motorbike – out of a basket! They are called 'basket bikes',' Harry explains, wiping away the sweat trickling down his bulky neck. 'Your bike came in a basket, too. The engine number shows that it belonged to an old army bike from 1972. They don't make that kind of engine any more. You are really lucky... in a couple of days you will see your beauty.'

It is a sunny day in January 1994. We are standing inside Rocky's workshop, a low shed made from corrugated metal sheets located at Sainik Farms, one of the suburbs of New Delhi. The shed is stuffed with all kinds of motorbike parts. Harry, a heavy set German biker, looks at the scene with a sparkle in his eyes. After three days of listening to him raving about the beauty of vintage bikes, I have some problems feigning enthusiasm. The heaps of rusty metal pieces thrown about the compound which reeks of engine oil and garbage in various stages of decay hold little attraction for me. And Harry going on and on about the duties of bikers, makes me wonder if buying an Enfield bullet was really the right thing to do.

'If you want to drive a bike, you first have to learn how to repair it. Every biker knows how to hold a screw driver and set the points. In Goa, you don't only have to learn to ride the bike, you also have to learn to service it,' Harry tells me with conviction. I look at my long fingernails and wonder how they will survive the ordeal ahead.

In the hot midday sun my mind starts to wander to the one question which brought me here: What am I doing with my life? When I celebrated my 30th birthday, I realized I was lingering at a crossroad. It was time to make up my mind: Should I continue following my career in journalism as a political correspondent for a German newspaper or should I choose motherhood? One thing I knew for sure. There was no way I could work long hours and weekends and be a good mother at the same time. As a mother I wanted to see my child grow, without the hassles of juggling a demanding profession with parenting.

Finally, destiny forced some action upon me. In January 1993 my friend Rosie invited me to visit Goa. She had rented a house in Anjuna with a spare bedroom and wanted me to join her. So I booked a flight and thoroughly enjoyed myself for two weeks. Although I had little in common with the drug consuming hippies I met in Anjuna, I enjoyed the beaches, the friendly atmosphere and I discovered my love for riding motorbikes. Most of all I loved the warm sun. Staying indoors through those long, cold European winters really depresses me.

Just before returning to Germany in 1993, I met Harry, who told me how little a used Enfield Bullet costs. Immediately a path opened up in my mind: I could take a two-year sabbatical from my work, buy a Bullet and ride through India while pondering what to choose: family or career.

Said and done – now I was sweating away in Rocky's dusty compound, listening to endless stories about motorbikes. Harry did not talk about anything else and Rocky, the owner of the place, a short man with a protruding belly, was happy to entertain him. Luckily his wife Swati was as bored with the subject as I was. On the third day of waiting for my bike to emerge from a basket she took me into her bungalow next to the bike shed. The interior was cooled by air conditioning. Marble floors and a built-in modern kitchen proved that business was going well. In the master bedroom Swati showed me her collection of pashmina shawls. Now this was something really interesting…

The following days I excused myself from visiting Rocky's work-shop. Instead I spent my days relaxing by the pool of the Imperial Hotel, taking a break from New Delhi's Tourist Camp, where I had joined Harry who liked this kind of surrounding. Already my existence as a pampered journalist seemed to slip away. In the basic huts of the Tourist Camp I got the taste of rough living on the road.

Five long days later my motorbike was ready. Harry had restored it in the original style of a Royal Enfield, with a chromed tank, red paint and golden lines, a classical beauty. When I first saw her, she took my breath away. I started to feel scared, really scared. How would I be able to handle these 170 kilograms of metal? 'You have to give her a name, you know. For a man a bike is female. We always speak of her, like speaking of a lover. But you are a woman, so I don't know how this works with you,' said Harry. Honestly, I had no idea. I kept on referring to my Bullet in my mind as 'the bike.' But a name? Luckily I had no problem with the gender. Clearly, this red and chrome beauty was female.

'By the way, in Goa I will introduce you to my friend Alberto. He will love you, tall and blond as you are. He is the best motorbike rider I know. He used to race motorbikes when he was young, a real gentleman from a good family in Milano. I don't really have the patience to teach you how to handle the Bullet. But he can show you how to ride a nice line.' Clearly, Harry had had enough of me. He was looking forward to spending time with the three bikes he had bought from Rocky.

One day later Harry got the bikes wrapped in straw and sack cloth. Following a lot of screamed orders a bunch of coolies lifted them on board of the train which took us directly from New Delhi to Belgaum. There he rented a truck which brought us to Goa. I had booked a room at Martha's breakfast home in Anjuna, where Harry and his friends met every morning.

Finally the Bullet was standing in front of my modest room. I was still scared. I hardly dared lift her off her stand for fear I would not be able to put her up again, let alone drive the beast. On the second evening in Goa, Harry had organized a dinner at a cozy little restaurant. His love for motorbikes is only equalled by his love for cashew feni which he likes to consume in one of the little bars that dot the Goan countryside. Thanks to Harry I came to know of hidden pockets of Goan culture like local restaurants that serve wild boar – far away from the tourist trail.

In one of these cozy restaurants, I finally met Alberto, a man with long hair held together in a ponytail, and a heart-warming smile. He was dressed in a stylish leather jacket. 'Show her your motorbike,' said Harry. 'You know, Alberto was one of the first to ride a fully modified Bullet with an elongated frame.'

During dinner Alberto and I kept on talking about everything under the stars except motorbikes. He told me about his past as a successful photographer and cameraman in advertising. 'I have worked with the best director in Italy, but the stress just takes the joy out of life. About 15 years now I am spending my winters in Goa. I love the warm climate. Of course I cannot follow a serious career this way, but having time is more important for me. Luckily, I can afford to live like this.'

The evening passes quickly and Alberto offers to drive me home. I hold on to him and he opens up the throttle. His bike is speeding across the road, I feel like I'm flying. In front of my room he kisses me on the cheek. 'It was a nice evening. I enjoyed talking with you. Unfortunately I have to leave in a week. My girlfriend and her son are waiting for me in Sydney. I have decided to live with them in Australia for a while. Sydney is the most beautiful city on earth, maybe I will settle there permanently.' This announcement hits me like a cold shower. Then I think: What did I expect after one evening of interesting talk? A commitment for a lifetime? Anyway I have to sort out my life. Falling in love would only divert me from this purpose.

Alberto spends most of his remaining days in Goa with me. He shows me how to handle the bike and I notice that there are different approaches to being a biker. 'I never touch a screw driver. That is what mechanics are for. If your bike needs repairing, bring it to a workshop. Hanuman is the best mechanic in Mapusa; I will introduce you to him. I've known him since he was a little boy.' Under Alberto's guidance I start riding my motorbike. I love the heavy rumble between my legs and I love the looks I receive when I pass all the shacks in Anjuna stuffed with Hippies.

The only problem is starting the bike's engine. I never have to ask Alberto to help me. After a few ineffective kicks from me he instantly turns up to launch my bike. My problems begin once he is gone. With a heavy heart I then have to deal with my Bullet alone. The riding I manage quite well but starting the engine remains a problem. I keep on kicking and kicking, but most of the times she simply refuses to spring to life. I usually have to ask somebody to help me get my bike underway.

I dread the minutes when I try kicking the bike in front of a chai shop, all eyes on me watching my fruitless efforts - how embarrassing. Even more humiliating are sometimes the responses from experienced bikers when I ask them for help. Some flatly refuse; some others pretend they don't hear me or they give me a response along these lines – 'If you want to ride a bike, you also have to start it.' Many times I am flabbergasted by the lack of courtesy and manners. If you want to be a hippie you have to forget being polite, it seems to me. I miss Alberto, the gentleman rider.

After six weeks of endless kicking my right knee is out of order. I cannot walk anymore and have to rest for some days. After these days of idleness my Bullet slowly gives up her resistance. I still don't have a name for her, but she slowly accepts me as her rider. Some patient kicking now starts her up.

Three months had passed in Goa, time to hit the road. Many of the people in Anjuna seemed only interested in consuming various kinds of drugs and hanging out on the beach – a way of life which for me was simply boring. I was ready for new experiences. So I packed my bags and mounted the Enfield, heading for the Himalayas.

I don't remember how many times I almost got killed on Indian roads. Trucks would swerve towards me. Jeeps almost hit me. Deep holes opened up in the middle of the road. In remote valleys of the Himalayas I fell into icy rivers while crossing them…but my Bullet took me everywhere. In Himachal Pradesh we visited McLeod Ganj, the exile home of the Dalai Lama. We participated at a Kalachakra, a tantric initiation, in Jispa, a little village in Himachal Pradesh. We rode through Rajasthan back down to Goa. We even spent two weeks at Osho's ashram in Pune.

I guess my guardian angel was very busy during the one and a half years I was riding through India. Throughout this time I shed many layers of my pampered personality. I learned to live with hardly any comfort and I lost my fear. My Bullet turned into my best friend. She seemed like a mamma to me, protecting me and keeping me safe.

When we returned to Goa, it felt like coming home. I loved the green hills and the coconut palms swaying in the breeze. The local people seemed to welcome me as well. Finally I could show the ones who had sneered at me that I truly was Bulletproof. After so much time on the road my bike mostly started at the first kick: no more humiliation in front of Chai shops, no more begging for help, no more snide remarks. Once again I took a room at Martha's breakfast home, because the owners were really friendly.

The weeks passed quickly with relaxing in the sunshine. Nobody seemed to hurry in Goa. To enjoy life seemed of utmost importance to everybody. Although I had experienced many adventures, the answer to my big question still eluded me. It was time to tell the newspaper if I would resume my position. Then, one sunny morning, there was a knock on my door. I opened it and there he was: Alberto, the gentleman biker.

'I am a free man now,' were his first words.

To cut a long story short. Alberto and I got married in 1997 in Milano, Italy and we decided to live in sunny Goa. One of the first things we did was to modify my bike into a rainbow coloured chopper. Finally I came to name her – Berta. In 1999 our son Valentino was born. Although many things have changed in Goa of late, after 15 happy years we still love to live here.

PHOTO: ALBERTO SANTORO

My Bullet named 'Berta', after the transformation.

Garv se kaho hum ghanti hain!

An outsider among the Goans

Vidyadhar Gadgil

Vidyadhar Gadgil is a hack who actually enjoys writing, but, being a contrarian, he prefers editing what others write. He has lived in Goa long enough to call it home, but, on the principle that home is sweetest when you are not in it, currently lives in Kathmandu.

It would be nice to be able to say that I fell in love with Goa at first sight, but actually I don't remember very much of my first visit to Goa. There were nine of us, nineteen-year-old college friends, who had come down for a week's vacation. Most of our time in Goa was spent completely drunk. To a bunch of students who could rarely afford to drink in Pune, the price of liquor in Goa was a revelation.

It would also be fun to do a scathing account of that trip, in true Hunter-Thompson Gonzo style, a kind of 'Fear and Loathing in Goa'. But the reality was rather more banal – or maybe my mind, in the interest of helping retain my self-esteem, has drawn a discreet veil over some of the more cringe-worthy episodes of that visit.

A drunken holiday in Goa is a kind of rite of passage for Indian youth. So we landed up in Goa by bus, found some cheap accommodation in Santa Cruz, and used that as the base for our drunken roving through Goa. I suppose we did most of the things that middle-class 19-year-old Indian students do on holidays in places like Goa. Wake up around 10 am, have some breakfast, start getting drunk or stoned, drift off to a beach, ogle some white women (at that time nudism was still common among foreign tourists at beaches like Anjuna), have a dip in the sea, keep drinking off and on, have dinner in Panjim, and back to the Santa Cruz dump for more drinking till the merry day draws to a close.

★ ★ ★

Some time ago, on one of my visits to Pune, I bumped into two of the friends from college who had come along for that trip, and they got into reminiscence mode when I told them I now live in Goa. Their memories were clearer than mine – they must have been far less drunk than I was, or their imaginations more fertile – and as the evening proceeded I kept trying to change the subject, but they were fixated on memories that were clearly among the highlights of the carefree days of their youth. A bunch of balding, greying, paunchy, middle-aged men getting nostalgic about the most extended drinking jag they had ever had in their lives: we must have made a strange sight.

The beach is one place in Goa which I avoid like the plague. Anything to avoid bumping into a tourist. When I think about this attitude of mine in relation to that first trip to Goa, it's obvious that the reason I don't go to tourist places in Goa is to avoid bumping into myself from a quarter-century ago. Not out of fear – we weren't dangerous, didn't have enough gumption to be – but out of shame. I still cringe when I think of my first visit to Goa, and am pretty glad that I don't remember much of it. Some things are truly best forgotten.

★ ★ ★

A few years later I came down to Goa for – you guessed it – a holiday, along with some friends, including my then girlfriend and soon-to-be wife. She is of Goan descent, and the family had kept up its links with Goa – a common phenomenon as I was to discover – with a magnificent, if dilapidated, family house which was opened up whenever any of the family came down to Goa. This trip was also a drunken affair – it's difficult to imagine a young Indian tourist for whom drinking like a fish doesn't figure heavily in the list of 'to-dos' in Goa. A little better than the previous trip, though – we were older, if not very much wiser, and it was a mixed-sex group. Also we were idealistically trying to live up to vague ideals of 'social and political commitment', which fortunately did not preclude staying drunk through the day.

Goa grows on you. My wife and I worked there for some time in the 1980s, and I suppose it got under our skins, which is what made us return here to settle down ten years later. And now it's 'home', even though we may not always live here. *Sossegado* is a reality in Goa – it's difficult to get anybody particularly excited about anything, and to get them to take some effort over it is even more difficult. People are friendly, and the natural beauty is something truly special. Over time I have developed a strong sentimental affection for the place.

But, after all, it's just another nice place, of which there is no shortage in the world. Why then do all these Goenkars get all misty-eyed and chauvinistic when they talk about Goa? My inability to comprehend something so obvious to most Goans shows why I am, and always will be, an outsider. 'Breathes there a man with soul so dead,' asks the poet – sure, and it's probably the perpetual outsider who is a misfit even at 'home'. Mea culpa!

My wife, fortunately or otherwise, refuses to play the 'Goan' game, always describing herself as a Bombay girl, since that is where she grew up. She has the one vital possession that is most needed to play the 'insider' game in Goa – ethnic Goan descent – but she is quite firm in staying out of the whole thing. And I can see her point. Goa is a cool place – in hipness if not weather – and this whole Goan identity business can get rather tedious.

★ ★ ★

My first brush with the psychopathology of being Goan was about three years after that. Being Goan can be quite a game, sometimes approaching art, and it demands a certain skill to play with panache, with a self-righteous moral outrage over the innumerable injustices heaped on Goans. The first time I worked and lived in Goa, in the mid-1980s, I was attending a meeting on environmental issues. I watched with admiration as this guy gave us a long lecture on how the benighted *bhaille* (Konkani for outsiders) were destroying Goa and are the cause of all its ills. He didn't even bother to talk much about environmental problems; that was not really germane to his tirade.

His chutzpah was something to admire: the guy isn't even a Goan but from Mangalore or Calcutta or somewhere like that. But his ethnic background had supplied him with a suitably Portuguese-sounding Catholic surname and that was enough, or so he believed. Later I asked him how he did it with such élan and style, and only got a blank stare in return. I still haven't figured out whether that stare indicated refusal to answer the question, or whether he was trying to snub me for my impertinence. But now I veer round to the view that he himself believed that he was Goan, whatever that may be. Good for him, but he's mistaken if he thinks the *niz* Goenkars are buying it.

In the Goenkar stakes, all that matters is ethnic background. If you can dig out some ancestor of yours who was of Goan descent, you're in. A quarter-Goan, half-British and quarter-anything-else woman who has lived in the UK all her life, and never come within sniffing distance of Goa, is by some mysterious process more Goan than a *bhaillo*, without any Goan blood, who has lived in Goa all his life.

If you think this is a bit of a joke, this line was laid down quite explicitly by the recently deceased doyen of Konkani literature Chandrakant Keni. Apparently he met this 'Goan' musician in Nainital, who could sing a mean song in Konkani when he was in his cups. The unfortunate fellow had never been to Goa, but what the hell – Keni and he rhapsodized about *Goenkarponn* through the evening. As to the alleged Goan whom Keni was introduced to that evening by the hotel receptionist, he was a Sikh who had lived in Goa for a mere 25 years. In the tale, as told by Keni, that was enough for Keni to dismiss the Sikh outright. Maybe the Sikh spoke perfect Konkani, maybe he had spent years doing social work in Goa, maybe he had worked hard to protect Goa's environmental and cultural heritage, its 'unique identity'. Keni doesn't bother to even think about it, and why should he? When the ethnic link is quite clearly missing, any claim can only be a carpetbagger trick.

★ ★ ★

There are *bhaille*, and then there are *ghantis*. A *bhaillo* is a generic term for people from outside Goa, and would include tourists, though well-heeled foreign tourists are of course *bhaille* of a special sort and fawned upon. *Ghanti* is a more nuanced term. Meaning 'from over the ghats', it is used for labour-class Maharashtrians and Kannadigas.

After hearing an exposition on the subject of the sins of the *ghantis* from the teenage son of a Goan friend, I protested and mentioned for good measure that I was a *ghanti* too. He was a trifle discomfited, but covered up, saying that he did not mean to disparage *me*. A little discussion revealed that if you are middle-class, Westernised and reasonably comfortable with English, you don't qualify to be a *ghanti* – you are just a plain *bhaillo*. Even here, declassing oneself is not an easy affair.

Bhaillo has also been acquiring delicious new flavours. Now this covers creatures like Delhi savages, nouveau-riche squatters, Bombayite carpetbaggers, and British expats looking to make a small pension stretch a little longer in a poor Third-World country. The idea being that all the moneybags from all over India and the world covet Goa and are buying it out from under the feet of the *niz* Goenkars (who seem to be in an almighty rush to sell out, but don't go there unless you want to get into a huge argument about how capitalist globalisation deprives people of choices and that Goans are therefore actually forced to sell).

Yet, Bihari, Jharkhandi and Oriya labourers, of whom there has been a sudden proliferation as the dubious joys of globalised capitalist development wash over Goa, are of course *ghantis*. It's a class thing.

And then there are *binktamkar* (mysteriously, this literally means 'one who sells groundnuts'). This term is more common in South Goa, and I haven't heard it too often or understood its origins, but you could get some explanations and lots of heated debate and invective by posting a query on Goanet.

★ ★ ★

If you feel like studying the insider-outsider debate in all its finery, you could do worse than visit the popular loony-bin that is Goanet (http://goanet.org), the mailgroup that claims over 11,000 subscribers. Or, if you feel like some adventures on the wild side, have a dekko at Goenchim Xapottam (http://groups.yahoo.com/group/GoenchimXapotam/).

Populated largely by non-resident Goans (NRGs), Goan identity and the need to save Goa from the *bhaillo* onslaught are topics of perennial interest on Goanet, and continue to be discussed threadbare ever since the mailgroup's inception over ten years ago.

As is only to be expected with any non-resident phenomenon, Goanet is largely about the right-wing NRG view of the world – the need to preserve the natural aesthetic of Goa so that the NRG visitor can continue to have a relatively unspoiled museum piece to visit, with its culture and environment intact. Goans who have made good in the West wax nostalgic about Goan culture and heritage and art and language, and so on and so forth, culminating smoothly into a discourse on how the *bhaille* have made a mess of the place, and need to be packed off forthwith.

As for Goenchim Xapottam, the attitude there is that there is nothing objectionable about abuse and invective. One of my bizarre memories of this mailgroup is of actually being called a 'Marxist *bhaillo* piece-of-shit mf'er', or something like that, on a public mailgroup. The notable affability and good nature of Goans is a ubiquitous but, obviously, not universal trait.

★ ★ ★

In school and college in Pune, Goans were not an unknown phenomenon. Studying in a Jesuit school, we had a few Goan Catholics in class. They were bundled off for Catechism classes while the rest of us revelled in the joy of chucking paper missiles at each other in Moral Science classes. With names like Mark D'Souza and Ronald Menezes, they were almost certainly Goans, and so it proved to be. These friends and acquaintances got carried over to college. I think we had a few Goan Hindus in class, but in a place like Pune, the Amonkars, Mashelkars, Kakodkars et al blended effortlessly into the Maharashtrian mass, and you couldn't really be sure – though I rather suspect that one Shankar Salelkar, who used to glower silently through the day on one of the back benches, was *certainly* a closet Goan.

In literature and Bollywood, the Goan character is inevitably Catholic, and it is difficult to imagine the Goan Hindu depicted with the Goan part of his identity made much of. For the rest of India, Goan means Catholic. For Goan Hindus outside Goa, the main interest in Goa is the fact that their traditional family deities are in Goa, so a regular pilgrimage is essential. Beyond that it doesn't really matter.

In Kiran Nagarkar's *Ravan and Eddie*, Ravan in Bombay lusts after the Goan Catholic women with their skirts and smoothly shaved legs. Maybe Freud (or, rather, Sudhir Kakar) would say Ravan craves the Westernised woman, represented by the Goan Catholic woman. A strictly dated concept – by the time we were in college, most middle-class girls unselfconsciously wore Western dress, and the Bengalis, Tamilians and Maharashtrians were as Westernised as the Goans. An attractive pair of legs peeping out of a skirt could be attached to just about any ethnic Indian sub-identity.

Is being perceived as Goan a purely Catholic phenomenon? Go figure. Goan chauvinism crosses all boundaries of religion and caste, but in the perception of the average Indian, all Goans are Catholic.

★ ★ ★

Does being 'Goan', however you define that, add some lustre to your reputation? Understandably, in Goa it seems to play such a role. But Goan artists and writers are also quite keen to claim various other writers and artists as Goan, and as vociferously exclude others. In a conversation with a friend, he spent quite a bit of time doing just this. 'Don't you find this exercise rather tedious,' I asked, 'after all, who cares whether an artist is from Goa or from Jhumritalayya, or whether the influences on him are Goan or Mesopotamian?'

My mistake, as I soon learnt. The Goan label automatically qualifies an artist as worthy of serious consideration. But the exercise can become specious, where any and every manifestation of an artist's work is analysed from the standpoint of its Goan-ness or otherwise. (In another twist, any achiever with a Goan Catholic-sounding name is claimed as one of Goa's very own, and proof of the innate superiority of Goans, as in the case of Freida Pinto, who happens to be Mangalorean.)

Are Goans significantly more hooked on this insider-outsider business than other communities? Probably not, but elsewhere your face is not rubbed in it anywhere near as much. In the modern metropolis, it's considered pretty much irrelevant.

From the other side of the divide, it's quite sad to see outsiders here make pathetic efforts to play the Goenkar game. The sensible ones just maintain a discreet silence when the conversation veers round to this topic (as it inevitably does); but far too many succumb to some kind of a desperate need to belong, and try to flaunt how much they're doing for Goa, thus implicitly qualifying as Goans. Doesn't work, and they might as well save themselves the effort.

And why would anybody want to belong to a particular ethnic group, unless one wants access to government patronage of some kind, or has some desperate need to belong – to something, to anything? The value of being an outsider is grossly underestimated – it's tremendously liberating. No weight of expectations, and you can treat all manifestations of ethnic chauvinism as anthropological case studies – and whine about them to your heart's content.

★ ★ ★

Goa has been colonised by India. Instead of granting Independence to Goa after the departure of the Portuguese, the imperialist Indians took over. Thereafter, they have been grinding the poor, innocent

Goans into the dust and enriching themselves. Only a new struggle for True Liberation can give Goans justice. Etc.

Next time you hear this, don't argue. Don't trot out all the obvious evidence against such a thesis. Not unless you want to spend a few hours in a futile argument. It isn't about logic or reason, but about emotion. Besides, if you're reasonably aware of what's happening in Goa right now, with big money from Delhi and Bombay buying up large chunks of Goa, you begin to see merits in the argument and that damps your patriotic fire.

As to Westerners – except for Russians, who are all branded as Mafia – they have not been conveniently pigeon-holed as yet. The Goan is as worshipful of white skin as the average Indian, and, after all, the *goras* are relatively rich.

★ ★ ★

This *Goenkar* business can leave outsiders feeling hurt if they've lived for a long time in Goa. Like my friend Vishram Gupte, novelist, who was telling me about how the outsider tag is used as a put-down against him every once in a while, even by Goans he considers to be close friends. A 'Don't get above yourself, we know what you really are' kind of thing. Sensitive soul that he is, this was hassling him no end.

Anyway, his sense of hurt had a productive outcome – he wrote a weekly column titled *Bhailyancho Saad* (Voice of the Outsider) in the Konkani newspaper *Sunaparant* for some months. I rather liked his fanciful idea of setting up an organisation of that name (especially for the play on Bailancho Saad, a well-known women's rights organisation in Goa). I suggested a motto: *Garv se kaho hum ghanti hain* (Say with pride we are outsiders). Trips easily off the tongue, having gained familiarity due to the ubiquitous Hindutva slogan, '*Garv se kaho hum Hindu hain*'.

Membership is currently open to all disgruntled *ghantis*.

★ ★ ★

My motorcycle had developed some major fault and I was forced to commute to work by bus for some days. The bus left every evening on the return journey, and it was crammed to the brim with labourers on their way back to their shacks in some village, after a sweaty, dirty day's work. Talk about the great unwashed – the journey was a complete nightmare as one rubbed shoulders and more with a tightly packed bunch of labourers. Bloody *ghantis*, I said to myself, and thrilled to that little frisson of joy that only fortunate insiders can experience in full measure – ethnic superiority and class superiority in one neat package.

Must remember to scratch *Grapes of Wrath* off my favourite books' list. What does Steinbeck know?

★ ★ ★

Being accepted as an insider, however provisionally, can be a frightening experience. At a meeting in our village on the Regional Plan, after the usual rants about how outsiders are messing up the place, one of the speakers (a good friend of mine) felt a little apologetic (or was provoked by the grin on my face), and said that we don't mean people like you – even though you may technically be outsiders, your hearts beat for Goa.

Thanks, but no, thanks! My heart beats well enough, Goa or no Goa, and when it stops, it stops. Besides, how dare anybody try and take away my coveted outsider status?

Garv se kaho hum ghanti hain!

Aniruddha Sen Gupta, *'Diamonds and dust', Panjim, Goa, 2011*

The teacher

Pamela D'Mello

As a journalist, Pamela D'Mello has been interpreting Goa for the national press, but now imagines she can expand her boundaries and interpret life itself!

Suresh bunched up all the mark sheets on his desk, slid them back into the plastic folder, adjusted his shirt and fished out a small comb from the back pocket of his trousers. He combed his wavy black hair, patted it down with his hand, then settled back into the hard wooden chair and waited. The parents had been called at nine that morning to collect the second midterm exam results of their wards. He checked his watch. Another fifteen minutes to go.

He glanced around the classroom. How silent it was now. The children had been given the day off for Open Day.

At this time every week morning, they'd have filled the small classroom, buzzing with talk. How they loved to chatter and play the fool. And constantly adjust the wooden benches and their bags and their legs. They were constantly fidgeting with the desks, all the time attempting to wrest more space for themselves in the cramped classroom. Little bickerings would occasionally erupt and annoy Suresh. But they were good natured tiffs, with none of the aggression of adulthood. Most of the jostling in the class broke out over space. He sympathised, but what could he do? There were forty three children in the small classroom. A few of the taller boys and girls were more than uncomfortable, their long legs cramped under the low benches. With no space for their large book laden knapsacks, Suresh had ordered everybody to put them down on the floor beside them.

This evinced howls of protest. 'But sir, the floor is dirty,' they cried in unison and he relented. So there they sat, two children and two bulging bags on a narrow bench, fussing and fidgeting while he attempted to get them enthusiastic about a civics lesson in self government.

They were not a bad lot, these children, thought Suresh. He enjoyed teaching them. If you shook off the pressure, you could not help liking them.

They were tolerant and compassionate in an innate way. Somewhere in adulthood, they would lose that. For now, they never sweated the small stuff. 'Sir, spelling mistake! Spelling mistake!' they would shout, when Suresh made the inevitable mistakes while scribbling in English on the blackboard. 'Ah, *voi, voi*, thank you,'-Suresh would reply, breaking into his native Konkani language, and sheepishly smile back at his class. They understood, they forgave his recurring spelling errors in the English language.

One thing he could say about these students, they were always in high spirits. None of the moodiness that afflicted adults. They teased each other good naturedly, gave their mates nick names, got into the occasional squabble, but through it all were a solid team, wresting as much fun and play as they could from the day. In spite of the adults around them. Tell them they had a free class period and could go out into the school compound to play and they'd be off in a blink, faces beaming the joy they felt. Cancel their outdoor physical education (read play time) class and they'd be utterly devastated.

He smiled at the *monickers* they gave each other.

'Oye Umesh *Umlo*,' one boy would be teased.

'Yes, Mister Chagas *Choricio*,' an unfazed Umesh would counter.

All part of the game. The teasing could lead to mock fights. Like Saddique '*Ponnos*' and Ishan '*Chonno*' who were always at it.

Those two could rarely sit still, just full of beans. Nothing serious, if you really looked at it, just irrepressible energy. Boys would be boys. They'd bait each other, spar playfully and before they knew it, one would accidentally get hit and a real fight would ensue. How often Suresh had walked into the class to find the two wrestling each other near the teacher's desk, while the other boys cheered and the girls sat watching, not sure if they should join the ruckus or play the part of demure young ladies increasingly expected of them.

He had half a mind to march them off to the school office, but something always held him back. The boys reminded him so much of himself as a boy - perpetually upto tricks in school and out. So, Suresh would stand them outside class for a period as punishment or make them write lines in their notebook – 'I will not disturb the class' – a hundred times. Off course none of it worked.

Not as clean and smartly dressed as the other middle class students, the two boys stood out. Suresh had heard they'd got into trouble with the Maths teacher once. He'd caught them showing off to the class a couple of snails and a caterpillar they'd captured in a matchbox.

Suresh had once been cornered about the two boys by the Maths teacher.

'Aren't you going to complain about them to the principal?' his colleague had enquired one afternoon in the staff room. 'You really must, you know. It will go against you. They like discipline here and teachers who can control the class,' he said.

'Oh, must I complain? All the classes get noisy when there's no teacher around. What's so special about my class?' Suresh responded.

'I'm just telling you,' the Maths teacher shrugged. 'The Principal already knows that class V A is a bit rowdy. '

Ishan and Saddique. What was he to do with them? If he complained to the Principal about their antics in class, they'd be in serious trouble. They were at the bottom of the class academically. Ishan's handwriting in English was barely legible. He had flunked in every subject except Hindi. Saddique was marginally better. He managed to clear

Konkani as well, possibly cramming up the answers like all the students did. Learning by rote was still the norm in most schools. The boys were Kannada speakers but had grappled with school in two alien languages – Konkani and English. Like the others they'd gone from learning Maths in Konkani, and then switched to English, thanks to the confounded system followed here. Like the others the numbers were probably all muddled up in their head. Some ingeniously devised form of torture this was.

So what could Suresh do? He'd have to break it to their parents today, that both would probably have to repeat the class. They'd fared badly throughout the year. There was no way they could progress to the next year, even if by some improbable magic they came up with brilliant papers at the final examination. The crimson lines on their report cards stood out like beacons. The parents had to be told, even though he knew the boys would probably get a tanning from their respective fathers.

Sure they had other talents. Saddique loved playing the standup comedian, and was good at it, seeing that he had the class in splits when he mimicked the latest Hindi film heroes. Ishan was great with his hands, a talent he probably inherited from his father, who was a carpenter. His craft projects for the school exhibition had won their class the first prize. But what did this count for? Nothing. Absolutely nothing. Without an SSC certificate, he'd never be able to escape his father's occupation and would end up like him – a carpenter.

He'd have to talk to their parents.

As expected, Suresh watched Ishan's father look at his son, his mouth thinning with displeasure, a dire warning in his eyes that said 'wait until you get back home'. How would a beating get a ten year old first generation learner to take to his studies? With no one to teach the boy at home, he probably went to the village tutors who held afternoon tuition for over twenty children at a time. A marginal improvement on the school class. In school the teachers barely had time to check if any of the forty students understood the lesson; everyone had to simply sprint ahead to complete the portion for that year. But what could Suresh do? Some things were just not his brief.

Monica's parents walked in. They were an odd couple, the mother a tall pretty woman in her late thirties. Widowed early, she had married a foreigner, a bald wiry white man around sixty, with a calm benign expression. Monica apparently liked her new father. He intervened when her mother scolded her all too often and was far more tolerant of her antics. He also enjoyed her chatter and did not consider her a pest. Now he stood leaning against the classroom wall, while her mother listened to Suresh complain about Monica's incessant chatter in class.

'She's like that only. Even at home, she's constantly disturbing her younger brother and won't let him study. I want to send her to boarding school,' said the mother, a frown marring her pretty face. Monica bowed her head and stared at her feet, her eyes avoiding the other parents and some of her classmates in the room.

'She's just naturally exuberant, there's no need to do anything hasty,' Suresh overheard the white stepfather say, as the family left the classroom.

The stepfather was probably right, thought Suresh. But what could he as a teacher do? The students had to conform. This was mass education. He had to maintain some order in the class and get on with the curriculum, or the principal would bring it up in the next meeting. It would be another strike against him. He was not even sure if he would be asked to continue at the year end.

Suspensions were rather routine here. The teachers had been strictly warned against hitting the children. But how did one control the class without some fear, thought Suresh. Especially the boys. In his days it had been easy enough, his teachers simply used the stick on the naughtier boys; and dealt out summary punishment. Instant justice, or instant injustice if you were really innocent and just caught in the crossfire of someone else's mischief.

Now it was different. A fifth standard boy had been suspended for a week, merely for playing hand cricket in the classroom. All the teachers knew that Jessica's parents had been asked to shift their child to another school, because the girl had once bought her mother's mobile to class, coupled with some other minor transgressions, that were brought up in justification. She had once brought a scarlet lipstick tube to class, applied it to her lips and collected the impression on a sheet of paper, sending the girls into giggles and her class teacher scurrying to the Principal's office, after she walked in on the scene. It had not helped Jessica's case that she wore the previous year's uniform to school, its hem well above the knee, or that the prefects had caught her twice wearing dangling earrings to school. All of it sacrilege!

Whether you agreed or disagreed with the suspensions, you kept your opinion to yourself. It was best that way, thought Suresh. No good would come from voicing an opinion. During his months at the school, he had noticed there were teachers who spoke kindly, understood and encouraged the students and never took misdemeanors to the Principal. In return they gained the loyalty, love and attention of their students, no matter what subject they taught. On the other hand, there were teachers who were feared.

He had his own matters to deal with. In addition to the academic reports, he was also obliged to give a conduct appraisal report on his students. 'Be honest and straight forward, it's all for the good of the students,' the principal had said as he collected the sheets from the office. It was a strange and intoxicating power teachers had, he mused. To make or to break.

A week after the final examination, Suresh found himself called to the Principal's office. The performance and conduct of all his students had been evaluated. Suresh had debated with himself, on what he should or should not leave out while writing the appraisal. It was particularly difficult in Saddique and Ishan's case. Should he mark them out or cover up? He had lost a night's sleep pondering over it. There was his own temporary tenure to consider. He needed the job and there were rules to be followed...

Entering the office, Suresh stopped. Ishan and Saddique's parents were in the office. His heart sank. Did it mean what he thought it did? Had his 'honest and straightforward' remarks about the two boys weighed so heavily against them? Were his evaluations to extract a heavy price? Surely, they were just coltish boys who needed some prodding and assistance to cope with their studies. He knew the school had little patience with misdemeanours. Maybe he should have omitted any mention of it. It was too late now.

The parents were told. . . . albeit gently.

'The boys do not fit in.'

'They are a little too rowdy for the school. The other children are not used to that.'

'We are sure there are other schools more suited to them.'

'They need more help. We are very sorry, but we have to manage a large school, and keep standards high. . . .'

The parents turned to him, expecting him to say something.

Suresh thought he saw pain and anger and accusation and resignation in their eyes. But they were wrong. It wasn't entirely his fault. He did not take that decision, the principal did. So why were they looking at him that way? He was just conforming to the school guidelines. What could he have done?

Leaving Dubai

Sheela Jaywant

Since there are no 'undo' or 'delete' buttons in life, Sheela Jaywant steps on plenty of 'ouches' and marches on regardless. She writes because otherwise words would burst out of her ears with all the things she's dying to tell everyone about. Believes you only live once and if you live right, once is enough.

Emigrants make great travellers. And preservers of tradition.

You could say Shambhu, though a Goan through and through, with the 'purest' genetic lineage, was a third generation expat.

His grandfather had left Palolem in the '40s, gone via Mumbai, Bhusaval and Ahmedabad to Jodhpur, Rajasthan, where he'd set up home in the outhouse of a local Thakur. His fish curries were complimented by all who shared a meal in the Thakur's huge house. Shambu's grandfather had never seen such big, bustling *kothis,* mansions in Goa. His cashew-studded *moonga shaak,* that elaborate recipe of turmeric yellow, coconut-milk based curried sprouts, was such a hit that he was invited more than once to the Umaid Bhavan, the Maharaja's palace, to prepare it. That, and the special vegetable stew, *khatkhate.*

Shambhu's father had to stay in Jodhpur to help out. Though he studied in the local school, he had to learn to read and write Marathi as well, to recite Sanskrit *shlokas.* Even so, Konkani was the only language spoken at home. Every other month, either father or son went to Goa to help with the farm work, care for an ailing elder or attend a wedding...and returned laden with ingredients like coconuts, *solan, trifala, papads, sandgem,* even pepper and the staple part of Goan cuisine – unpolished 'boiled' rice or *ukdde tandull.* Once a year, at *chavath,* for the Ganesh festival towards the end of the monsoons, both paid the mandatory visit to the village together. All five of Shambhu's grandmother's deliveries were in Goa; Shambu's father knew of his siblings, their arrival and progress, only through telegrams. He had to stay in Jodhpur to help his father, the only one to do so. Yet, as the eldest, it was his duty to 'look after' the younger ones in Goa.

Shambhu's father was clever, and in his teens, he ran away from *his* father (they weren't really close anyway) to Mumbai. He couldn't run from his responsibilities though, and he had to send money home to feed and educate the rest of the clan. He lived in a *chawl,* worked as a cook, and the community living drew him closer to his roots than ever before. After marriage, he took a ship to Dubai, where he got a job in a kitchen attached to a nursing home – Al Reem Polyclinic and Hospital, at Al Rafa.

He was an active member of the Goan Club, played football for the Canacona Team there, and made only Goan friends. His wife had stayed behind in Mumbai, but once their two children arrived, she went to Goa where Shambhu's father had earned enough to buy himself a small flat in a corner of Panaji. It was easy to scrounge and save in the early years. He shared lodging with other Goan workers in Dubai, they cooked food together, ate together, played and laughed together. Quarrels were sorted out by the elders and penalties were strictly enforced. Discipline ruled. Of the fiscal kind, too. He could send money and come 'home' once a year. Indeed, Dubai was a kind of heaven.

By the time his children were of school-going age, he had taken a flat on rent and transferred his family to Dubai, too. His wife took up a part-time job in a grocer's shop owned by a Keralite, and added to the income. After that, brothers, cousins, extended family members, all migrated to Dubai in rapid succession one by one, to prosperity and to a dream come true. And the visits to Goa were reduced to once every couple of years. By air, for ships were no longer practical. Not that it mattered, for there was little to go to Goa for – from dried mackerels to the small, red *alsande* beans, from the beaten rice, *phoa,* to fresh curry leaves, everything was readily available here. Every festival was celebrated with gusto – Sankrant, Shimgo, Ganapati, Dussehra, Diwali, and for the Catholics, Easter and Christmas, as they did back in the villages.

Shambhu, therefore, though he grew up in Dubai, knew himself as a 'Goan', though he had been to Goa but twice before his marriage. All his friends and all his parents' friends were Goan. He spoke Konkani at home like all other Goans he knew. He did have other friends, either Malayalis or Maharashtrians, but his closest pals were Goan, out of habit. Yet, he knew little of Goa, other than what he heard from his mother and others, because even his father seemed to know very little of the place he was so intensely loyal to. That loyalty was passed from generation to generation, geographical location notwithstanding. Goans who had come from Africa, Goans who had come from Pakistan, there was a cohesion amongst them. Catholics and Hindus kept their distance, there was a space between the two Goan communities, but to the world they were one.

Shambhu answered his tenth board exams at one of the schools run by the Indian Government, a Kendriya Vidyalaya in Dubai, and was dispatched to Goa to complete the twelfth standard and then on to a diploma. Those three years were a miserable experience. Goa wasn't the land of milk and honey of his dreams. The hostel was cramped. His room-mates expected him to pay for everything and even stole things from him because he was from Dubai, hence 'rich'. The camaraderie that he'd seen all his life in the Dubai *goenkars* was lacking here. Maybe they had it amongst themselves, but he was a *bhaillo,* an outsider. Instead of *bhakri,* they ate pizzas. They smoked and drank like no one in Dubai did. Shambhu tried making friends with the quieter ones and finally settled in, but Goa was no longer 'home' and he was happy to return to Dubai, certificates in hand, ready to start work as a laboratory technician.

Back in Dubai, he took up a job in the same hospital where his father worked. For Shambhu, Dubai had *parampara,* tradition. Stability.

Romance. Marriage. A separate home, not too far from his parents and his siblings. Children. He changed jobs, took a better paying one in a chemist's shop. Life was good.

Until 2008. Almost overnight, the chemist's shop shut down. Recession, they said. He tried getting back to Al Reem Hospital, but they weren't hiring. Within a month, he was forced to take a decision: this place was not his home. Here, he really was a bhaillo. Without a job, without money, he couldn't stay here. He was trembling as they packed to leave the UAE, the only place that he was familiar with.

He kept mumbling, '*Deva Parsurama*, God Parsurama, hope everything goes well.'

His wife, Sushila, ever supportive, comforted him. 'Why won't it? Stop being so negative. Where are the passports?'

'The tickets, the luggage, the gold, everything's in place. But I'm so afraid. I hope everything goes well.'

'Stop fidgeting. We're lucky, at least we have a home to go to.'

'It's only Baba's flat.'

'Only? Do you have any idea how expensive land is in Goa? But Hari mama said we could go and look around and we'll get something cheap.'

'I don't know that, but we have our ancestral house, too, in Canacona. Baba said we could go there. But what job will I get there? I can't do farming. In any case, the farms have been sold and they're living off that money, I heard.'

'We can't go there, all your cousins, their children, there will be objections.'

'I've helped them, haven't I, when they needed cash for the *moonjas*, the thread ceremonies of their boys? For their daughters' dowries? For repairing the roof? Getting the toilets indoors?'

'Get real. You think they remember all that? Think it matters?'

For three generations, no one from Shambhu's immediate family had lived in Goa. They had known Goa through their parents' memories and the stories the elders in the community had narrated. They had preserved traditions zealously. In a foreign land. They didn't marry outside their caste, they didn't mix with 'others'. They felt safe, comforted with their own. They sang folk songs, play-acted *tiatrs,* made *kismur* and *kodi* and *tausali.* Shambhu knew that in Goa things were different. The newspapers carried stories of fratricide, rape, theft, cheating. They ate *paneer* and *chola-bhatura* and *noodles* at weddings. He knew that without bribing, nothing moved. He'd seen it, witnessed it, and feared it. Sushila, born, nurtured and educated in Dubai, was innocent. To her, Goa was 'what to tell you, the best place on the planet' as her parents...no, grandparents had told her. Now they were leaving their brick and mortar dwelling for their virtual home, Goa. They had phoned the cousins, informed uncles, transferred funds... time to reverse-migrate.

★ ★ ★

The flight has landed at Vasco. The pre-paid taxi driver speaks Hindi and asks them which hotel they want to go to. On the way, Shambhu sees a sign-board: an estate-agent's shop. He halts the taxi for a minute to step inside it. He steels himself. He has a strong instinct for survival. He has to 'do something' and he knows he'll do it. The same Goan blood that made his grandfather step out to a better future runs through his veins. It's time to relocate. No more glittering lights, no sky-scrapers, no malls. It's time to adjust.

Shambhu takes Durga-Mangesh's name – he'll do it.

Sweet voices smiling

Cecil Pinto

Cecil Pinto dabbles in many diverse activities to make a living, while remaining consistent in producing his unique brand of Goa-centric humour writing. Cecil claims to be 'world famous all over Goa' and is not too keen on expanding these horizons, while sipping his beloved Caju Feni and observing the ways of the world.

St. Thomas Church, Aldona. 25th May 1996,

5.47 p.m. In a few minutes I'm going to enter the church and exchange rings and wedding vows with Beatrice. But for now I wait with Dad, Mom and Conrad about fifteen meters away from the entrance to the church. The long white decorated wedding car has dropped us off. The earlier Saturday Mass has not yet ended. The golden glow of the setting sun gives a nice warmth to everything. On our left flows the Mandovi river. Fortunately our backs are to the cemetery which has the ominous phrase '*Aiz Mhaka Faleam Tuka*' over the gate – 'Today it's me, tomorrow it will be you.'

I look at the imposing façade of the freshly whitewashed church and wonder why nobody has written a book examining the unique façades of each church in Goa. The lovely bandstand stands on my right unused, except on the rare occasion of a grand feast or funeral. Maybe it could be decorated and used as the waiting place for grooms and brides-to-be?

'Mum, where's Beatrice? I thought the car had picked her up first?'

'She's already in the sacristy side corridor of the church and will join us with her entourage, just before everyone enters the church. It's bad luck to see your bride before that.'

I wonder what Beatrice's dress is like, since I have no idea what she, the flower girls, and the pageboys will be wearing. That was one set of decisions among the many I was glad to let go. I also wonder where

exactly in the church corridor Beatrice is standing with her family. Our
Aldona church is famous for giant murals on those particular corridor
walls. One depicts Life-in-Heaven, the other Horrors-of-Hell and the
last one shows what-happens-to-those-who-don't-receive-Extreme-Unc-
tion. I wonder which would be the appropriate backdrop for a bride to-
be. My bride.

> *I see the church, I see the people.*
> *Your folks and mine, happy and smiling.*
> *And I can hear sweet voices singing,*
> *Ave Maria. Ave Maria.*

I look around outside the church, glad to see more guests arriving.
Although I myself rarely attend nuptial ceremonies, it's a nice feeling to
have your people around. There's Aunty Bridget, Uncle Justin, Judy, John
and the gang come from Mumbai just for this. And there's Sheila,
Anthony, Blaze and Aileen. And there's Eric and Lydia. And Carmelita,
Pyarelal and Praveen. And Lily Aunty and her husband and her trendy
niece down from Bahrain. I don't recall her being invited but she will add
glamour to the reception if she is as good a dancer as Lily Aunty claims.
Her risqué outfit is already the subject of much attention. And there's
Caru Titiu, never quite the same since Filsu Mai died. And Julie, Patrick
and Connie. And Monica and Mrs. Mendes. Most of them are familiar
with this church and exude a sort of confidence in being on home territory.

Huddled nearby, or ambling around in close groups are Beatrice's
relatives and neighbours, curiously checking out everything not similar
to their home turf. William, Orlinda, Simpho, Nilu. Where's Ivy? Oh
yes, she's one of the flower girls. Wonder what colour dresses they finally
chose. And there's John, Gracy and Ilito. Bushun and Bolu are also flower
girls. I still don't know what their actual names are. And I see some of
Beatrice's neighbours from Divar, and relatives from Majorda, whose
names I don't know either, but the faces are familiar. I smile at them but

they look away. Maybe that too is a pre-nuptial custom? 'Thou doesn't smile at thy to-be spouse's folks.'

In the distance I recall seeing my friend Levitte approaching and then here he is at my side. I ask Levitte how he came and he says by bus. All the way from Porvorim. That's what friends are for. Relatives sometimes participate because they have to. Friends because they want to.

My best man, Conrad, is also my younger brother. His lifestyle, and hence dressing, is rather unconventional and this is his first ever suit. But he seems to have taken to it easily. I'm okay with my suit but am glad that I refused to wear gloves. Levitte lights up a cigarette. I wonder whether it is appropriate for me too to smoke a cigarette to kill time. Mom seems to know what I'm thinking and signals 'No!'

I am beginning to feel extremely self- conscious. My recently married friend Tony had warned me about this.

'You're going to be King for a day.'

'That's good, no?'

'Everything you do will be closely scrutinized.'

'Oh!'

I see two more close friends, Neelam and Thomas, approaching on my Yamaha motorcycle. I last saw them around noon at Panjim where I left them at the reception hall to oversee the decorations being put up. They look as though they set up and sampled the bar too. No problem. A little drink never did anyone harm. I could do with a stiff one right now myself. They tell me all is well at the hall. Neelam wants to take my bike to go home to Sanquelim to change and return for the reception. Sure pal, go ahead. Today I got myself a white air-conditioned car for a hundred and twenty kilometres, or 1 a.m., whichever comes first.

Gracy approaches my Mom. This is Beatrice's elder sister. Some discussion occurs. She goes back into the church corridor and comes back. More back and forth, and gesturing, and I know something is wrong. Dad sits astride a friend's bike and comes back in a few minutes with a bunch of tightly bound red roses. Everyone seems relieved.

I enquire. Mum tells me that this bunch of roses had been sent along with some other stuff from Panjim. Mum assumed they were surplus flowers from the hall décor, sent for use at home and so she had just dumped them in a vase. Turns out that this bunch of roses was the avante garde bridal bouquet that Beatrice's florist friend had made. We don't recommend her services any more.

> *You by my side, that's how I see us*
> *I close my eyes and I can see us*
> *We're on our way to say 'I do'*
> *My secret dreams have all come true.*

The people from the previous mass are leaving. The bells are pealing. My time is approaching. I see Fr. Felix at the entrance. Ah, Fr. Felix. The only priest I could think of to handle this most important religious ceremony of my life. I recall our conversation during the preparatory course.

'Father, and when do we say – "I do"?'

'You don't.'

'Huh?'

'You read out your vows to each other. That "I do" part has long been discarded, since people started getting literate.'

'And you're telling me that we walk down the aisle together? But I thought I wait at the altar and she's brought up the aisle by the best man?'

'That's passé too, Cecil. You walk up the aisle together as equal partners in this relationship.'

'So they don't play "Here comes the bride" anymore either?'

'No Cecil, you've been watching too many soap opera weddings on TV!'

'Beatrice would like "Ave Maria" to be played as we enter.'

'Good choice!'

> *Oh my love, my love, this can really be.*
> *That some day you'll walk, down the aisle with me.*

Let it be, make it be, that I'm the one for you.
I'd be yours, all yours, now and forever.

And suddenly it is the time. The choir starts playing. From around the corner I see Beatrice's mother approaching. I mouth the word 'Mai!' She sees me and smiles broadly, which is reassuring in this sea of serious faces. Following her, rounding the corner in sequence, appear the cute little page boys, flower girls and the bridesmaid – all dressed in red and black combinations. And then there she is. Beatrice. My Beatrice. Looking absolutely radiant. She lifts up her veil looks into my eyes and her serious countenance breaks into a faint smile. My heart misses many beats. I can't help but smile broadly.

Everyone present has converged at the entrance of the church. The smiles are contagious and in seconds no one has a serious face anymore. Bushun and Ivy are even self-consciously chuckling to themselves as little girls will do.

'Shh!' says Orlinda to them.

'Let them be,' says Fr. Felix, 'This is a happy occasion!'

These words act like triggers, opening a floodgate of smiles all over again. A huge weight has been lifted off my shoulders. I no longer feel compelled to look serious and frown. Is it because I am no longer the singular centre of attraction? Is it because everyone's smiling? I don't know. It feels very good. Beatrice too seems a little less tense.

Fr. Felix stands at the entrance and says some very profound words before inviting us in - couple and crowd. I don't really listen to what he is saying. I have ears and eyes only for my lovely confident smiling bride. We hold hands. Our fingers grip each others lightly. Together we step inside the church where the choir has by now grown much louder.

I see us now, your hand in my hand.
This is the hour, this is the moment.
And I can hear sweet voices singing
Ave Maria, Ave Maria

Village vibes

Melinda Coutinho Powell

Desperate housewife Melinda Powell used to fly the world's skies. These days you are more likely to find her in the comfort of her garden chair, surrounded by her children and dogs, documenting life on the ground, one day at a time.

In the summer of 1998 my husband David

and I relocated from Mumbai to Goa. We ended up building a house next door to my mother in Chaddo Vaddo, Davorlim. When we were scouting around for good locations to build a house, beachfront properties were available at a steal but we chose to reside in this village because of family ties. Don't you know of the notorious 'Thakkar brothers' murder that took place in Davorlim, they asked us incredulously. Watch out for those migrants who congregate at the village junction, they warned us. Undaunted we took the plunge and settled down in this tiny hamlet.

Settling down had its fair share of woes. We were viewed with curiosity because of David's 'non-Goan' status and our city connections. Stories circulated that these fancy '*Bomboikars*' would not survive here. To add to it, my two German Shepherds Alf and Shadow barked their heads off at anyone who attempted to visit us. So we were viewed from a distance with scepticism and there was endless speculation about our lifestyle. Our twins Lisa and Rebecca cycled with the kids in the neighbourhood and played with them. Through our interactions with people at the village market, we gradually 'sort of' got accepted by the village folk. Today I've made my adjustments and they have made theirs. They have learnt to respect my privacy and I in turn have learnt to ask them appropriate questions when I meet them: *Have you got a letter from your son in the Gulf? Is there fish in the market today?*

My village has a meandering road lined with gulmohar and jaca-randa trees. Old houses that have stood the test of time stand majesti-cally, displaying grace and dignity. In the centre of the village stands the white-washed St Joseph's chapel and a large village square where all public functions are held. The chapel is the hub of social and religious activity. The foyer is a great place to catch up on village news – *Filomen Aunty slipped and broke her leg while feeding the pigs!... Joeboy has returned from Dubai with a Filipina bride!* No modern methods of communication are needed; flash messages are passed on instantly.

The feast of St Joseph is celebrated in the month of May – fire crackers and bombs explode at dawn to herald the special novena Mass at the chapel. This feast is a tradition which is celebrated with great pomp. Every household lays out a mouth watering spread of traditional cuisine and the aroma of tangy *sorpotels* and *vindaloos* wafts in the air. Relatives from far and wide are invited and there is a lot of merriment and laughter. And of course a heavy consumption of *feni*.

My village consists mainly of senior citizens, women, children and, as in many Goan villages, comparatively fewer men. The non-resident males mostly work on cruise liners or in the Middle East. The women are capable and resilient; besides looking after their home and kids, they supervise house repairs, drive cars confidently, handle their banking effi-ciently and are quite internet-savvy. The women of the village also take pride in their homes and gardens. Many households rear pigs and hens and most compost their garbage.

Demographically we do have changes. A few 'outsiders' have bought property in the village and they are in the process of constructing houses. A few Goan landlords have built tenements and they rent out rooms to migrant labour. Earlier we could recognize every passer-by, today we don't. Change is inevitable. A lot has happened since I moved to Goa ten years ago.

Goa has approximately 347 villages, where the majority of the Goan population resides. The outside world often mentions Goa in terms of rave parties, trance music, beach side bashes and Russian and Israeli communes. But that is just a slice of life in some tourism-affected coastal areas. The real heart and soul of Goa is found in the villages, where people are warm and friendly, where neighbours will lend a helping hand in times of trouble, where there are long lasting friendships that span generations. Of course there are family feuds too, but by and large, people are sincere and affectionate. All manner of Indian festivals and feasts are celebrated in the village. Traditions and customs bond village folk together. There is a certain dignity and decency which is portrayed in relationships.

Our village is made up of a motley bunch of characters: Dona Imelda for instance is a frail, silver-haired woman with a wizened countenance. All her sons and daughters live abroad and she is looked after by Vitozine, the adopted daughter who stayed behind to care for her. Dona Imelda is a permanent fixture in her balcão. She chats animatedly to passers-by, pronouncing judgments on several village issues. Old as she is, with her sharp memory, she knows every villager's family tree down to the grandchildren's names. She is consulted on marital problems, property disputes and she even gives recipes to newly married brides. One often sees her dozing in her rocking chair, rosary in hand.

Then there is Pedru the plumber, a bespectacled comic-looking man who roams around on a rickety scooter with a bag of odd-looking tools. His nick name is *English Pedru* because he insists on speaking a strange dialect of English with Konkani words thrown in. Pedru does not have a formal degree in plumbing but he will undauntedly tackle any plumbing task with an air of wisdom. While on the job, he will regale you with tales of how he has worked in the houses of landed gentry and how his services are sought after far and wide. While leaving, Pedru never fails to give me tips on how to bring up my children – he has a brood of nine. His exit line is always – *You trouble, you phone for me.*

And then there is Philomena, my gardener, who looks after several gardens in the village. She is a thin scrawny lady, who walks around with an air of determination. Ask her how old she is and she will give you a different answer every time. She is like a magician in the garden, silently trimming plants, weeding and pruning. Widowed early in life, she now supports two drunken sons who regularly beat her up. Yet she walks with her head held high, living with an undying faith in God and a hope that her situation will improve one day. Her courage and fortitude are an encouragement to all.

How can I forget our Jack of all trades – Manuel, the village shop-keeper. Manuel runs a small *posro* at the entrance of the village. He has jars of different shapes and sizes, huge sacks of pulses and grain. He sells all kinds of groceries, he even has a license to sell kerosene. Rumour has it that he plans to stock petrol as well. His shop is a maze but ask him for anything and he will pull it out from some corner. And of course he will painstakingly wrap every purchase in newspaper, tied up with string. His specialty is home repairs: be it a fan to be fixed, masonry work to be done, roof tiles to be fitted, Manuel is your man. Manuel loves to talk and he loves to gossip. His imagination runs riot as he conjures up colourful stories on each house in the village.

Our village has a Consumer and Civic forum that disseminates a lot of useful information to everyone. It has organized cooking gas safety camps as well as awareness meetings on different issues. The villagers managed to get a resolution passed against mega housing projects in the Gram Sabha. We have been fortunate in that since our village keeps a generally low profile; no builders have set their sights on local property yet. We also have a weekend village medical clinic that is supported by a generous non-resident from the U.S. Treatment is free and every week-end you will find a queue of senior citizens waiting there for blood pressure check-ups and for advice on minor ailments.

As I look back on the past ten years of life in my village, scenes of unity and togetherness flash though my mind. When my father passed away some years ago, all the neighbours came in and took charge of funeral arrangements. They made endless cups of tea for visitors, they spent time with us and offered prayers. Various families took turns to send us food. I will never forget their help in those troubled times. We have a buddy system, no one is left stranded. If there are disputes, the elders of the village try to sort them out amicably.

When I sit sipping tea in my garden in the early morning, I enjoy the melodious sounds of different species of birds. Many a time I've spotted kingfishers, brahminy kites and swallow-tail magpies. As I watch yellow buttercups swaying gently in the breeze, an inner peace fills my soul.

Rural Goa is changing but one can still find age-old customs and traditions prevalent in many parts. We still have freshly made *pau* delivered by a *poder* on a cycle and the fisherman still does his rounds, selling small catch to the villagers. Not only are the fields in the village still being cultivated, but all kinds of leafy vegetables, pumpkins, cucumbers are grown organically on a large tract of land. We have a village tavern where the locals drop in at any time of the day, where arm wrestling contests and regular brawls abound!

As a child I remember seeing long stretches of white virgin beaches, vast expanses of verdant fields and forested hills all over Goa. Today hillsides have been ravaged to make way for housing complexes and fields have been filled with mud and built upon. The Goan identity too is under fierce attack and suddenly everyone feels vulnerable to 'outsider' invasion. Indians from other states as well as foreigners have chosen to make Goa their home. Many middle-aged people are choosing to retire in this beautiful state. Goa has a certain magical charm that attracts and beckons people to its shores. Writers as well as artists have chosen to make this their home. Home is where the heart is. My heart is in my village. I wonder how long my village will remain relatively untouched. Until the inevitable happens, I shall enjoy the sylvan setting, camaraderie and all the sights and sounds that make up village life.

From the outside... in

Helene Derkin Menezes

Helene Derkin Menezes likes her humour like her martinis — very, very dry. When she isn't pounding away at her keyboard in the land of words, you will find her sticking something in the oven or reading aloud to her children. She abhors people who litter and loves prawn curry, Goan style.

The soft knock on the boardroom door

distracts me just for a second as I place the story board on the narrow ledge – custom made so that all can see the latest effort of the creative department.

It's Lisa, the Managing Director's secretary. 'Urgent phone call, H.' I nod at her and excuse myself from the client meeting; Fi's on the line. Fi is my tallest female friend; she must be five ten, easily six feet tall in stilettos, which she wears often. This is the nineties after all and in Soho, W1, London it's all about power dressing and labels. Fi and I are planning our holiday. St Lucia. Le Sport, for seven days of pampering and over indulgence, and boy do I need it. Working for the country's leading financial marketing and advertising agency means simply – work hard, party harder. The hours are long and often closed by a cocktail or three before the journey home, ready to do it all over again the next day.

'What do you think of Goa?'

'Where? What are you talking about, Fi?' I cast a wary glance back at the boardroom door.

'Goa... Nick says he can get us a really good deal there, a week for quarter of the price we are paying for St Lucia.'

'Nick? Who the hell is Nick? I don't want to go to India, I don't even own a rucksack, and I hate the smell of patchouli. I want pampering!'

Turns out Nick is the travel agent and he has convinced Fi that
after the recent plague scares in India, Goa is going really cheap. For me
India is a hippy destination, somewhere you go to find yourself – hot,
smelly and dusty with no credit card provision or whiff of Harvey Nics.
Not only that, you need time to explore somewhere as vast as India,
don't you? A week just doesn't cut it.

I call my well travelled parents while Fi holds on the other line.
Mum convinces me, 'You'll love it, it is like the Caribbean but the people
are nicer, and the food is fantastic! Go – you won't regret it.' Turns out
Mum and Dad have been twice!

'Go on then, book it,' I tell Fi. Not knowing the impact those words
will have on the rest of my life. I replace the phone and go back to the
clients. By the time my meeting is finished there's another message from
Fi, not only has the holiday price gone down again, but Nick's giving us
two weeks for the price of one, B&B, allocation on arrival, and we're
leaving in four days! This is to be my first (and last) charter holiday.

It is a chilly grey day in October 1994. The wind chill factor is high
and the temperature a shivery nine degrees when we leave Gatwick Airport for the sub continent. I am well travelled but this is my first charter
flight. I can't believe how tiny the seats are, so many loud people squashed
in, and this journey is going to take us twelve hours! We stopover in the
Gulf to stretch our legs and get our malaria medicine from Duty Free.
Fi's granddad was stationed in the tropics and swears that a paracetamol
and a shot of brandy are all you need every night to keep mosquitoes at
bay. Neither of us really likes brandy and there's a special offer on vodka
so we settle on a bottle to ward off the fatal disease. We land at Dabolim
Airport, stand in endless queues, have our passports and visas checked
about twenty times, every twenty paces, by what looks like the same man
dressed in khaki. We finally collect our bags and step out into what feels
like a sauna.

The sights, sounds and smells of India are like no other place on earth. We feel totally alien in our dark winter clothes. We find a rep and give her our names; she looks at both of us quizzically and tells us to wait over to the side, away from the other guests. I am paranoid, there's something about the way she keeps looking down her lists and glancing at us. Anyway, we wait. And we wait. Finally when all the other tourists are packed onto coaches and on their way, another flustered rep bundles us into a taxi, saying, 'Bob Malley right?' The door slams and we are on our way.

'That bloody Nick! Bob Malley! Crikey, it's a reggae commune or something! We are probably being abducted and sold! I bet you anything we are being taken to an ashram or worse a campsite,' I whine. I don't have the chance to whimper for long, the taxi ride soon brings me back to earth.

There seem to be absolutely no rules of the road here. A truck hurtles towards us on our side of the road. Rather than brake or pull over, our driver heads straight for the truck and actually floors the pedal to increase speed. 'We're gonna die!' we both scream. A miracle – the truck gets on his side of the road and our driver carries on as if nothing has happened. We take a right turn down a potholed road, adjacent to a railway track, navigating pigs, dogs and cows on the loose, down into a small fishing village. We slow down and suddenly the sparkle of the Arabian Sea hits me. 'Bob Malley' is a beautiful little cove called Bogmalo, and we are heading to a quaint white guest house right on the beach. We are both speechless. It's stunning. There are some fishermen casting their nets, no one else around, not even from the ugly four star hotel at the other end of the cove, no sunbeds on the golden sand, no noisy tourists from the plane – we are in paradise! Our room is freshly painted white, with a colourful bedspread, spotlessly clean. We dump our bags, tear off the London layers of dark clothing as if we're possessed, pull on our swimsuits, run to the sandy beach like two little kids and dive into the warm surf.

We don't realise then that we are the first ever residents to this little guesthouse which was formerly a family run restaurant. We ask about the name of the property and find it is named after the owner Nelo's dad – 'Jose' and his mum 'Etelvina' – a marriage of names resulted in 'Joets'. The bar and restaurant overlook the bay and the rooms are attached to the rear. There are a few nervous young men about the place who don't know where to look when we try to talk to them. At first we aren't quite sure who works there and who doesn't. They are shy and not used to talking to foreign girls, least of all when they are scantily clad in swimwear. But we are carefree; we've escaped from gloomy, cold Blighty where it's all central heating, tights, hats, gloves and scarves – to thirty two degrees of heaven where to wear anything more than the bare minimum is simply sacrilege to the sunshine.

There are no tables in the restaurant and we can't get a cold drink as there's no fridge either. From the noise there's obviously building

Joet's: a view from across the beach.

work and painting going on in the other rooms. A couple of days pass and though we are in paradise, there are a couple of mishaps in our room. Nothing major. A light fitting comes out of the wall and when we flush the loo it seems to flush the floor at the same time. And there are men asleep outside our room with nothing but tea towels wrapped around their waists! We are two street savvy girls from London so we aren't easily unnerved, but these guys sleeping in the corridor have us wondering what on earth is going on. (In the UK labourers do a nine to five and certainly don't sleep on the premises even if they do sleep on the job!) We have no idea they are working every hour God sends to finish off the pending work for Joets' first tourist season.

All is quiet in Bogmalo and we have barely seen another soul. Fi and I easily fall into holiday mode. She meditating and getting at one with the Goan vibe, and me with a bag of books. I am up at the bar sampling something called 'palm feni' which is brewed in the village, when she dashes up the steps saying, 'I've just met an Indian from Hampstead and he is called Derrick!' To which I reply that it's impossible, no Indians are called Derrick. She gets a drink and we have a chat about what we are going to do during our stay. One thing is unanimous, both palm and cashew 'feni' will take many samplings to get used to...

We like our little guesthouse and the guys around seem to be really pleasant and are trying their best to get things ready. The missing elements are slowly appearing but it is not yet what is clearly stated in the brochure. We both agree they are not quite ready for business. One of the tea towel chaps is painting a wall a brilliant white at the bar. We have our eye on the four star down the other end of the bay. Armed with the holiday brochure we set out to meet the area manager of the charter company we booked with.

The taxi takes ages to get to Panjim, the road full of holes, dogs, cows and goats that all need slow and careful navigation, though our driver obviously doesn't think so. We go at breakneck speed overtaking on blind corners, indicating left and turning right! Fi and I hold hands and say a prayer to as many Gods as are listening, we have never been on a journey like this – the ride from the airport was tame compared to the NH17.

It takes a while to locate the office in the capital, Panjim; we eventually find it above a Punjabi restaurant and meet the manager, a Scottish girl called Lynn who has beautiful long thick strawberry blonde hair. We relate our tale, telling her it is not the boys' fault, they are trying their best but the owners are just not ready for guests. I put on my advertising hat and say the guesthouse is just not what it claims in the brochure so they are breaking ASA regulations; Fi chips in that we like the beach there so could she just move us along to the four star please? We of course have no idea that she knows we booked this holiday last minute and got it at a knockdown price. The brochure rate is four times what we paid. Lynn says she is really sorry, she knows the boys at Joets, she will have a word and in the meantime she offers us a complimentary overnight trip to Palolem to experience sleeping in huts on the beach to help pacify us... if things aren't better when we get back she will see what she can do. But no way she's going to move us into the four star, it will be another guest house in the north. We want to go to Palolem anyway so this seems like a fair deal.

We take a look around Panjim trying to absorb the culture and not look too amazed at how different from home everything is. Feeling rather like outsiders from the attention we are getting, we then realise we are staring as much as the locals are looking at us and we try to blend in. Not easy, we are used to dogs on leads, cows fenced in fields and pigs in sties; men and women in suits and children with shoes on. And perfect fruit and vegetables immaculately cleaned on shelves in supermarkets along with row upon row of items we buy but never really need. This market scene is so alien to us. The ladies with their laden baskets upon their heads walk with as much poise and grace as girls in finishing school. In the fish market the ladies with their legs spread around their wares heckle for customers. The smell everywhere is overwhelming. We walk past the flower sellers enjoying the greeting of bright blooms and perfume. We stare astonished at the barber conducting magic on his customer with a cut throat razor, then gently massaging his head. We squeak when the barber is suddenly thumping him all over, the customer unfazed by what looks like an attack rather than a treatment. We take it all in. We have lunch at a local joint, this is nothing like the Indian food we have back home. The fish curry we order has our taste buds popping on our tongues like fat in water. We guzzle lime sodas to pacify our tongues and quench our thirst. We can't get over the cost of the meal, comparing it to the crazy London prices we are used to paying.

We head back to the south. The cab often brakes and we're thrown forward off our seats. The driver seems to keep his thumb continually on the horn and it soon becomes apparent the only use he has for the rear view mirror is to check his reflection. We are incredulous when we have to stop and pay a toll, when the road is in such an appalling state. When we are not shrieking in terror at this totally new approach to traffic sense we are laughing nonstop at the difference of it all. When we arrive back there isn't a workman in sight and the restaurant area has tables and chairs set up! We order drinks and sit and soak in the glorious sunset while gassing about the adventure of our day and what we would need for our trip further south the following day.

Suddenly Fi shrieks – 'There he is! That's the Indian from Hampstead!' I turn round and the world stands still. I feel myself blush and turn back to Fi. I gulp on my drink – the next thing we hear is 'hello girls' and are greeted by a huge grin of nutmeg skin and large white teeth. Turns out his name really *is* Derrick and he's just back from spending the summer at his aunt's house in Hampstead. He buys us both another drink and chats amiably with us. I don't think I have ever met a man who smiles so much. During the conversation he asks us if we would like to go to a church dance at Colva with him the day after tomorrow. Fi and I look at each other...church dance? Neither of us has ever been to a church dance, but what the hell? Fi says yes before I have time to think about it. He goes off to the bar and chats for a while to some guys dressed in football jerseys. He waves to us as he hops into a black jeep and drives off along the track that edges the beach.

The next day after a fantastic lunch of fresh prawn curry and rice washed down with more 'feni' (that would blow our socks off if we were wearing any) we are picked up for our trip to Palolem. By now we are slightly hardened to the 'road rules', and manage to take in the view without thinking it's the last thing we will ever see. Palolem is idyllic. The little camp is well geared up to take care of our needs. Our hut has little hammock style beds and is set just yards from the breaking ocean. We laze around, read our books and go out on a local canoe to fish but we are far more interested in the dolphins that follow us breaking the water gently as they rise to say hello. In the evening there's a barbeque and camp fire. We move away from the few other tourists and sit under the stars, drinking in their delicate light, watching the phosphorescent waves breaking a short distance away. We feel a million miles away from the stress and strain of the west end of London. This is nirvana. How can something so simple be so indulgent?

We are brought down to the reality of India when we arrive back to Joets to find a small white and brown dog with a broken leg hopping about the place –- apparently one of the drunken fishermen had thrown a stone at it. We are horrified but no one seems very bothered. There is no RSPCA to call and the guys at the bar don't seem to think the poor thing warrants a vet. We are both very upset. We know there are plenty of stray animals here and this is a country that is more concerned with feeding its growing population than the welfare of a stray but we can't help but feel sad and helpless.

As we wonder what to do we see someone out on the water, windsurfing. Fi and I both sail so we decide to ask Derrick about hiring a sailing boat when we meet him later at the dance. There doesn't seem much we can do for the little dog so it is with slightly heavy hearts we set out that night.

Derrick picks us up in his jeep with a friend in tow and we set off for dinner before the dance. Fi and I still have no idea what to expect. We stop at Colva and have dinner at the Longuinhos hotel. We listen to *mandos*, sung in the local language – Konkani. The conversation flows, like the drinks, with an ease that we are growing rapidly used too and I wonder if we will actually bother to make it to this church dance or not. Not that it matters, we are all enjoying ourselves. We tell the story of the little dog and Derrick says we can take it to the vet in his Gypsy tomorrow, while he is at work.

Then out of the blue I hear western music blaring out nearby and frown in annoyance - don't want to be reminded of home. I recognise the song, it's in the top ten back in the UK. Derrick says the dance must have started and Fi and I exchange glances – we are sure we're in for some very staid and dreary music as we drive up to the venue, but by the sheer volume of what's being played that is obviously not the case. The dance is called 'Noite de Fama' traditionally held on the day of the Colva church feast. I walk inside the cloth barrier vowing not to be so judgemental. What I thought was recorded music is actually a live band called Lynx, we are astonished – how can a bunch of Goan guys sound exactly like Take That one minute and Big Mountain the next!

The crowd is throbbing, these Goans are certainly not shy about dancing and not the foot-shuffling-arms-flinging stuff we know – this is the real deal. Around us in the most diverse fashion statements, in a rainbow of hues from saris to puff sleeve ensembles (not the designer labels and street fashion we were used to seeing), people dance. Partners dance ballroom style, and dance well – neither of us has ever witnessed anything like this before. All this is happening under a blanket of a million stars. Back home you feel like a lottery winner if you can go out in the summer without a coat on and here we are in the middle of the night revelling in the barmy weather in our sun dresses. It's a beautiful night, great music, good food, fine company - great conversation and lots of laughing. We all dance under those stars.

The sun is just waking up as we get back to Joets. We go back to our room though I am on too much of a high to sleep, my mind is on the tall dark handsome man who has swept me off my feet... 'Oo Baby I Love Your Way' reverberates in my head as I relive our slow dance together.

Later that day Derrick drops off his Gypsy for us to take the little dog to the vet. I can't believe I'm going to negotiate that traffic and those roads but that pitiful little pup has broken our hearts with his limping about, his eyes give me the courage to do it. We somehow find the vet, and come away three thousand rupees poorer – the vet saw us coming a mile away. But it doesn't matter. 'Puppy' is now on the mend.

The rest of the holiday flies by with Derrick making daily appearances, showing us around the little state he is obviously very proud of and we feel so at home in. Everywhere we go someone seems to know the smiling Derrick, we learn he's a windsurfer, it's him we see out in the bay everyday, practising for the forthcoming Nationals. We ask him about a boat and he says he can arrange it. Fi feels sick on the day arranged to go sailing so Derrick and I set out on the surf alone. We sail out toward Grande and Bat Islands, he knows how to handle a boat alright and we zoom along catching the wind, we tack and gybe like we have sailed together for years, the salt spray cools our smiling faces and time disappears like the sea horses on the crest of the waves. Eventually we rest in the petite secluded bay locally known as Santare and while the water gently kisses the sides of the boat we steal our first kiss under the warmth of the Goan sunshine.

When our fortnight in the sun is over and Derrick takes us to the airport, I don't want to go home. I tell Fi, 'I'm not coming, I love it here and I really, really like this guy, I am going to stay'. Derrick is the voice of reason (and panic, he has another girlfriend arriving on my landing flight!) telling me he isn't going anywhere... 'Go home, make sure it's not the sun and the palm trees you've fallen for'.

Poor Fi has to put up with me sobbing on the flight, I just can't believe I'm leaving the man or the place. Five weeks later I have rented out my house, handed in my notice at work, said goodbye to my family and friends in the UK and am flying back to Goa!

It's my first Christmas in India. On Christmas Eve Derrick phones my dad in England and asks his permission to marry me. On February 14th we are civilly married followed by a surprise party in the tiny cove of Santare where we first kissed. In April we get married in the beautiful Mae de Deus church in Saligao. We have a fairy tale reception at the Taj hotel and Lynx plays 'Oo Baby I Love Your Way' as our first dance. Lynn and Nelo are among our guests. Turns out that Lynn had phoned her fiancé Nelo from the office and read him the riot act for not having everything ready at Joets, their first joint venture. Nelo consequently phoned his friend Derrick to help him by getting Fi and me out of the way so he could finish up the work and get back into good books with Lynn!

The plan worked. Joets is still one of the best kept and well run guesthouses in Goa. These days Lynn and I are great friends, our daughters are in the same class at school. Fi travels often to Goa and thanks to the internet we are in touch on a daily basis. I don't think anyone, least of all me, dreamed that by trying to get an upgrade meant I would fall in love, leave my past life behind and never ever want to leave...

The scarecrow
in the woods

Mario Coelho

Mario Coelho likes seeing people laugh and smile, free of malice, hate and guile. He loves to dance, and act, and sing, he likes just doing his very own thing. He loves children, and adults who are kids as well, there are so many tales he'd like to tell...

In the village of Khotalli, in the sunny state
of Goa,

A warm and friendly province, where life's a wee bit slower,
There lived a farmer Damu, who had fields of fruit and grain,
Bananas and pineapple, nachnim and sugarcane.

Old Damu was the meanest man the town had ever known,
Unkind and ill-tempered, with a heart carved out of stone,
Most of all, he hated children, animals and birds,
He'd chase them off his farmstead with shouts and filthy words!

He had no family of his own, for he had never wed,
(They said he was so nasty he had horns atop his head),
He'd take potshots at trespassers who broke into his farm,
He'd pepper them with pellets and shoot a leg or arm!

The birds that lived around his farm would often for a treat
Fly into his fields and peck the sugarcane so sweet,
The mean old man would stamp and yell, and shoo them all away,
But the pesky little creatures would return the following day!

The rats and squirrels, mice and monkeys got in on the act,
(Everyone feels hungry – now, isn't that a fact?)
At sunrise, Farmer Damu would bewilderingly stare,
At his fields of rice and cane, now all raggedy and bare!

The farmer made a promise as he grinned a nasty grin,
That this titanic contest he simply had to win,
'I'll build a frightful scarecrow that'll scare them off for good!'
He muttered to himself as he whittled logs of wood.

He whistled as he set about collecting bales of straw,
To make a giant scarecrow that would terrify and awe,
'Just one glimpse of him will make them vanish in a flash!'
'Then I'll have my fields,' he laughed, 'and loads and loads of cash!'

A pumpkin for the scarecrow's head, his hair was made of straw,
Raisins in potatoes made his eyes, so that he saw,
A shiny carrot for his nose, a mouth outlined with chalk,
Wooden poles for arms and legs, so he could stand and walk.

An old straw hat atop his head, a red and white striped shirt,
A dark brown jacket for effect, begrimed with soot and dirt,
Patched-up trousers for each leg, a pair of canvas shoes,
(Full of holes and out-of-date, they'd long outlived their use.)

But hey! Instead of looking stern, the scarecrow smiled and smiled,
That laughing, beaming, warm expression got the farmer riled!
He did his best to rub the smile right off the scarecrow's face,
But the more he rubbed, the more it grew, at an even faster pace!

Damu, in a temper, gave the scarecrow's nose a tweak
And glared at him forbiddingly, 'You feeble-minded freak!
You can smile the whole day long – just scare those silly birds away,
I'm keeping you to guard my farm throughout the night and day!'

With that he picked the scarecrow up and marched into his field.
'Now listen here, Potato-face, just keep those eyeballs peeled!'
He thundered menacingly, as he slammed him in the dirt,
'Just do your job!' he warned again, 'Or I shall lose my shirt!'

And so the scarecrow stood on guard all through the day and night,
And towered like a steeple, a most sinister sight,
Now scarecrows, everybody knows, are scary, mean and vile,
But this one beamed from ear to ear – a bright, disarming smile!

The pigeons flew in for a peep and stayed on for a chat,
The sparrows, crows and egrets came and settled on his hat,
The mice showed up, the squirrels too, the bees came in a swarm,
And clustered round the scarecrow, who was affable and warm.

He told them tales of far-off lands, of pixies, gnomes and elves,
For he himself was magical (that's what they told themselves),
He chuckled as the monkeys danced, and sang the latest hits,
He told them little anecdotes that had them all in splits!

'We'll call you Khushal!' they announced, 'Because you laugh a lot,
Of all our friends, you're easily the jolliest one we've got!'
And so the scarecrow joined the club of animals and birds,
Who told him tales of jungle life and hung onto his words.

Damu checking out his crops one day, found his farm a mess,
To add insult to injury, the club was playing chess,
He spied the broken stalks of cane all scattered on the ground,
'I'll make that scarecrow pay for this!' he muttered as he frowned.

Angry and resentful, the farmer raised his cane,
And smacked the scarecrow's pumpkin head, so that he yelped in pain,
'I'll beat you black and blue,' he growled, and raised the stick once more,
'You were supposed to guard my crops, I've told you that before!'

He aimed another mighty blow at poor Khushal's head,
But found to his surprise, he had to save *himself* instead,
For Khushal's mates came charging in to save their friend from harm,
Oh, what a fight that must have been – the scrimmage at the farm!

The crows attacked the farmer's hat, pecking holes into the crown,
The squirrels pummeled his behind (they really went to town!)
The monkeys jumped onto his back and let fly with their fists,
The rabbits grabbed old Damu's stick and gave his leg a twist!

The farmer dropped his knobbly cane and fled for dear life,
(If he had had a family, he'd have run home to his wife)
The Club of Little Creatures celebrated long and loud,
And gave themselves a great big pat – they'd done their playmate proud!

'We'd best retreat into the woods, old Damu might return!'
A lively monkey called and quipped, 'This meeting stands adjourned!'
They dashed across the fields, their laughter ringing in the breeze,
Onto a narrow pathway that meandered through the trees.

They scampered deep into the woods, a jubilant parade,
And stopped at last to catch their breath in a warm and sunny glade,
'This is your new home, Khushal!' a bright woodpecker twittered,
Khushal's face beamed even more, his raisin eyeballs glittered!

And so the scarecrow lived contentedly among the beasts and birds,
The rodents, all became his friends, and the roaming forest herds.
Of buffalo, bison, leopard, deer, porcupine and boar,
They came to chew the fat, and tell him tales of jungle lore!

The weeks went by, and Khushal dwelt serenely in his hut,
Open to all forest beings, his doors were never shut,
The Club of Little Creatures came together thrice a week,
He had them rolling in the aisles (Khushal had a comic streak!)

And then one day they bustled in with terror in their eyes,
The sky was blushing pink, the sun was just about to rise,
'The hunting season has begun and there's no place to hide,
We'll all be killed… you've got to help!' unitedly they cried!

Khushal quickly rose; he dashed the slumber from his eyes,
His kindly heart responded to their panic-stricken cries,
His fertile brain began to tick; he came up with a plan
Smart enough to outwit any homicidal man!

They sat down in a circle: scarecrow, bird and beast,
Of every hue and shape and size, from the noblest to the least,
From buffalo, boar and bison, to squirrel, fox and hare,
They sat down quietly side by side and bowed their heads in prayer.

They listened with attention as their friend outlined the plot
And shouted with conviction, 'Let's give it our best shot!'
Resurgent and united, the club prepared for war,
Boosted by the courage of the scarecrow made of straw!

Silently the regiment of woodland creatures crept
Into the grumpy farmer's house, while Damu soundly slept,
They came out with an overcoat, voluminous and long,
A black top hat, a pair of drums and a shiny yellow gong!

The farmer'd been a drummer in his wild and carefree youth,
He still played now and then, although much longer in the tooth,
The gong was bought decades ago, when Damu was a boy,
He'd bang it up and down the house, beside himself with joy!

They crept into the garage (they'd found the farmer's keys),
And piled into the tractor (my, that was quite a squeeze!)
Leopard, bison, rabbit, squirrel, porcupine and deer,
The cheeky monkey at the wheel – they set off with a cheer!

They bounced along the twisting, narrow, rutted forest track,
And shuddered to a halt outside the scarecrow's rustic shack,
He hopped onto the tractor seat and raised a wooden fist,
And with a jolt they sallied forth, the enemy to resist!

Khushal quickly donned old Damu's European coat,
Assisted by his bearded friend, a sprightly mountain goat,
The top hat perched atop his head, he stood upon the tractor,
A tall, menacing figure and a strong deciding factor!

Now picture, if you please, the sound and fury in the wood,
As the tractor thundered headlong, and the giant scarecrow stood,
Like a bloodthirsty vampire or a supernatural bat,
In his flapping jet-black overcoat and towering black hat!

The antelope and buffaloes thundered past on either side,
The wild boar and the leopards matched them stride for stride,
The thunder of their hoof-prints resonated strong and loud,
As they swept past in a cavalcade – a rowdy, motley crowd!

The booming of the drums could be heard a mile away,
As the pair of drummer bears came together in the fray,
The forest hills resounded with the clanging of the gong,
As the troop of creatures galloped to a rousing Goan song!

The hunters in their clearing heard the thunderous sound,
Of a thousand heavy hoof-prints pounding hard upon the ground,
They clutched their high-tech rifles and looked around in fear
As the single–minded army of animals drew near!

Khushal, on the tractor, gave the signal to the troops,
In the twinkling of an eye, they diverged into four groups,
Crashing through the bushes, they converged upon the spot
Where the hunters quaked and trembled, too confused to fire a shot!

The fury and commotion made the hunters' blood run cold,
And Khushal, in his vampire cloak, was frightful to behold,
The beaming, sunny smile had disappeared from his face,
(A red-letter occasion, this, a very special case!)

The porcupines unleashed their quills; the leopards roared out loud,
The shadows of the evening merged and formed a great, big cloud,
The bulbuls, kites, and swallows swooped down swiftly from the skies
And targeted the startled men with shrill, discordant cries!

The hunters dropped their hunting gear and bolted from the glade,
Shaken to the very core, their nerves ragged and frayed,
They sprinted through the forest, vowing never to return,
From hunters to the hunted – how the tables had been turned!

The victory was accomplished; it was time to celebrate,
The cries of joy and triumph made the woods reverberate,
Khushal, hoisted high upon the shoulders of the crowd,
Felt warm and proud and happy, now *he'd* done his playmates proud!

The Fellowship of Creatures lived together without fear,
Hereafter, no predator ever dared to venture near,
Khushal, in his little hut, resided like a king,
A friend to every living soul - the scarecrow with zing!

And as for Farmer Damu, well, he found himself a wife,
Who kept him warm and happy, and endowed him with new life,
Gazing at his fields one day, his heart began to melt,
It dawned on him belatedly how the woodland creatures felt.

Ashamed of his behaviour, he sought to make amends,
So he slipped into the forest and met Khushal and his friends,
He came to visit frequently, sometimes in pouring rain,
Bearing gifts of rice and fruit, and stalks of sugarcane.

The kindly woodland creatures welcomed him into their fold,
A brand new friend and playmate, a man once mean and cold,
And if at times you might perceive his farm seemed like a mess,
You'd find the farmer with the scarecrow and the squirrels playing chess!

On the steps of pure flesh

Mafalda Mimoso
Translated from the Portuguese
by **Isabel de Santa Rita Vas**

It is said that one can always see Mafalda Mimoso vividly in what she writes but she has always sought to hide herself behind her words. Intellectual indiscretion is celebrated in her real and artistic life.

He stopped her midword:
She needed to speak there, in sounds, eyeless,
Of what moves and uplifts her.
She did not speak. Incapable.
It was no moral shame
It was fear of waste.
It was no insecurity
It was imminent collapse.
Earthy and carnal
He speaks, she acts.
High and deep
He is not accessible to be known,
That is how she thinks him, feels him.

From the skin and the moaning
From the words that are imperative
And from the fingers dug in,
She opens her legs to come out of herself.
An immeasurable step
Always beyond,
Stretching every limit.

He kissed her with diverse kisses
Kisses she stored in little boxes
Kisses she knows she cannot contain
She felt her breasts full and tense.
She remembered bits of herself
Unable to self dominate.

She entered him
Full of pleasure

She held him from within
In present domination
Controlling here.
Ever enjoying
Even though in her hands.

He plays with her
Direct and mordant
She slips on the curves
Of the brains, carefree
Loose, happy.

It is on the body,
That vehicle of other gods
That narrow pathway
That synallagmatic ritual,
That everything stops

Before

They are lifted up
In the eyes
Climbing the steps
Of pure flesh.

In Goa, like in some other magic places in the world where inspiration comes from in and out of us, women can be born from inside a tree, mature linked to it and live there forever.

Mafalda Mimoso, *'Goan Woman', Porvorim, Goa, 2007*

A village named Destiny

Vivek Menezes

For his entire adult life, Vivek Menezes (b. 1968) has been threatening to write a book. It's true that his essays and photographs are widely published, but it's not the same thing and he knows it.

In classical Greek, 'Moira' means fate, destiny.

The Goan village that bears this poetic name spills pleasantly over a series of hillocks, and is renowned throughout the region for the quality of its outsized bananas, as well as the eccentricity of its citizens. In every way, it is an archetypical village from the Old Conquests, the part of this territory that was occupied first and experienced the longest European colonisation in history. Like Goa itself, Moira has managed to sustain a remarkable cultural integrity into the new millennium, but now faces an uncertain future in an era of rapid change, demographic displacement and the erosion of hard-won social and political balance. On a moody overcast day in the monsoon season, I roared around Moira on the back of an Enfield Bullet piloted by my friend, Augusto Pinto, to compile a photographic portrait of the village for the newly formed Moira-Net Internet group. The results depict a little village in transition, trying to face down overwhelming forces. What will be Moira's destiny?

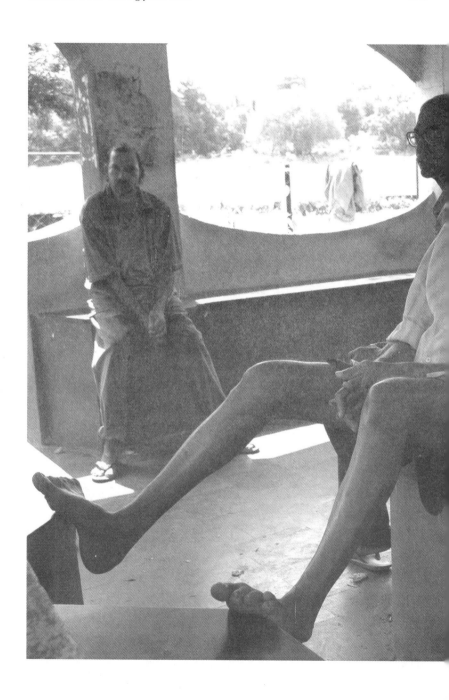

One still here

Aimee Ginsburg

Aimee Ginsburg has been living in India for close to fourteen years (ten of them in Goa) with two sons and an ever growing population of lizards, snakes, scorpions and other delightful creatures. She serves as the India correspondent for 'Yedioth Achronoth', Israel's most widely read newspaper, and other international publications.

I fell in love with Catarina Da Orta the

same year I smuggled a pair of my Grandmother's candlesticks, wrapped
in a pashmina shawl, out of grey Cincinnati, back to the old world. I
stood them on a wooden Kashmiri pedestal in my crumbling little house
in this land of coconuts and countless shades of green; of afternoon naps
and evening breezes; of blood red hibiscus, the juiciest mangoes. The
land where I started lighting Shabbat candles again, the land where
Catarina Da Orta was burned at the stake because, like me, she couldn't
let go of being Jewish, even if she tried.

I don't know what Catarina's Hebrew name was, her real name, a
dangerous secret they had to hide at all times. But sometimes I am
there with her as her Mama braids her hair back in Portugal, her old
country, singing quietly as she gently ties red ribbons through the plaits.
Sometimes I am with her while her husband oils her back, her shoulders,
and he whispers to her, lips close up against her ear: Channa Rachel they
are calling her then, I can hear it so vividly I am sure it must be true. My
Grandma's Yiddish name was Reizel, but that was back in the shtetl, in
Russia; she has been Rose to everyone since she landed with her family
at Ellis Island at the age of twelve. Grandma Rose's older brothers Ben
and Morris had gone on many years before them to start their new life,
far from the constant pogroms. When they met their family at port they
might have twirled their little sister round and round, her fiery red hair

flying, finally safe in her big brothers' arms. One brother had been mur-
dered on the journey, and the immigration officers at Ellis Island had
sent her sister Goldie – who had had polio – right back to Europe.
Grandma never wanted to talk about that.

The boat carrying Catarina Da Orta docked at port in Portuguese
ruled Old Goa, approximately 500 years ago. She was met by her big
brother Garcia (Gavriel? Gershon?) who had come here years before and
had sent for her, promising an easier life than was possible in Portugal at
the time. 'Besides,' he had said, 'Best we marry my two daughters to your
two sons.' What he meant was that it would be safer that way, The Secret kept shut tight inside their little family, and she agreed. When she
came to shore with her husband and boys it might have been late afternoon; slaves from Africa were bargaining with Hindu fishermen, over-
dressed white madams were flirting with Muslim merchants, tempted by
their silks and impeccable charms. The Inquisition would not reach here
for ten years, so meanwhile, although still careful to pretend at all times
(chicken sausages made to smell like pork, Sabbath candles lit in deep
dark inner rooms), the Da Ortas were safe. That first afternoon, Catarina
(Channa Rachel) may have rested just one moment in her brother's
embrace, the waters of the Mandovi River aflame in the light of the
setting sun.

I love watching sunsets over the Mandovi River, where its foamy
mouth meets the silvery teal of the Arabian Sea. I like to imagine that
Catarina used to do this as well: a longish sit on a rock or a log, saline
breeze on open face, mind gone blank for just a while. Like Catarina, I
am and always will be a stranger in these parts, and I wonder endlessly at
my voluntary exile, scanning the horizon, waiting for a summons, a sign.

I found out about Catarina while researching the 'conversos' in
Goa, those Jews who lived outwardly as Catholics to avoid expulsion,
persecution, and death by the Inquisition in Spain, Portugal, or their
territories. It was shocking to find out that a cruel Inquisition had taken

place in Goa, hedonistic heaven, traveller's delight. St. Francis Xavier-Goa's unofficial patron saint- had requested Lisbon to send the Inquisition here as his parting gift to the colony in 1552, and they did. It has been mostly forgotten, its severity almost always denied.

I loved Catarina Da Orta the first time I saw her name, and spent the better part of the year searching for clues about her life. By night, I scoured the Internet and corresponded by email with learned scholars in Portugal, Florida, Israel and Brazil. By day, I rode my ancient Honda Kinetic through heat waves and monsoon showers to the village of Porvorim, where I sat for hours in the Jesuit Library, dusty yellow books piled high, my clothes and hair perpetually damp. It was during that year that I began at last to reside in Goa, but in a long ago Goa, the home of Catarina Da Orta, and this dislocated me in a whole new way, a foreigner now in time as well as in place.

Catarina is really only mentioned, if at all, as a brief footnote to her brother's life: Garcia Da Orta, the famous adventurous physician, friend of nawabs and rajas, smugglers and slaves, whose book on the medicinal plants of South Asia is one of the best ever written on the topic. There is much to know about him, but not much we are certain about his sister: Garcia was a great favorite of the Portuguese governors and noblemen, so the Inquisitioners waited until he died before they arrested her. They tortured Catarina for nearly two years and then burned her. In the end, she had confessed to everything; to Yom Kippur, to the '*Shma Yisrael*' (the basic and essential Jewish invocation to God), to Shabbat. Hundreds of pages of her 'testimonials' are on file in an archive in Lisbon. Do they offer answers to my urgent questions? Why didn't she leave long before her arrest? There were safe places for Jews right outside the Goan border. In Cochin and in Madras, grand communities of Jews lived prosperous and peaceful lives. What was it that kept her in Goa despite her dangerous secret? I've tried to ask her, to warn her to get out, but my voice does not reach her in time.

Crowds of hundreds watched as Catarina burned outside the main cathedral, and when eleven more years had passed, they pulled out her brother's bones from his grave and burned them as well. Catarina (in standard Inquisition etiquette) had been given a chance to accept Jesus Christ at the stake in return for the mercy of a quick strangling before burning. She refused; she chose the flames.

★ ★ ★

The last time I visited my Grandma Rose, in my home town Cincinnati, Ohio, she was 96 years old and would live for another seven months. By then, her dementia was extreme. I was with her in the hospital one evening, everyone else had gone home. I had finished rubbing her feet with the cream that she loved and it was time for me to go. When I kissed her good bye, she panicked. 'But what about me?' she asked, 'where am I going?' 'This is a hospital, Gramma,' I answered, 'you are staying here, and we will be back in the morning.' 'But who *are* you?' she asked, and after I explained she exclaimed (this was the first time it happened, and I will never forget the terror in her eyes), 'But I don't know who I am! Who *am* I?' You are Rose Mayers, I answered, but this wasn't any help.

It happened to me once, not knowing who I am. I was in the Sinai desert, on a month long solitary retreat, in a period of time when my 'seeking' was all consuming. For the past week, I had been sleeping out on the sand dunes, on a small cotton rug and a sleeping bag; my small straw hut felt confining, separating me from the enormous intimate Spirit that was talking to me by then day and night. I would light a small twig fire in a pit dug effortlessly in the sand and fall asleep while watching the stars, billions of them, the Red Sea below me slithery black. On that special morning, (Shabbat, I later realized), I awoke as usual to the pre-dawn cry from the far away mosque – 'Allah hu Akbar!' (God is great). For one eternal, blissful moment, there was sky, there was sand, there was sweet sound of waves lapping the shore; there were no names, no words, no 'I'. But, then the question arose: 'Who am I then? Who is this experiencing it all? What is my name?' and as I came out of my reverie I felt awe but was quite shaken, and I knew I had taken all of this far enough for now. I walked until I found some people, wrapped in shawls, hair tangled and sleep in their eyes. They gave me tea, some biscuits, and we sat quietly together and watched the rising sun.

My Grandma Rose didn't know how to talk about God, even though she wanted to. She considered herself a practical woman, good at keeping books, at getting things done. She was beautiful, elegant, we thought of her as our queen. The first time I tried to talk with her about God she only said 'wouldn't it be wonderful to have faith? I always feel so jealous of those who do, but – I don't, so – what to do?' She told everyone that she really only kept kosher because her daughter, my mom, came home one day from the Hebrew school she attended, when she was about eight and 'put her foot down'. 'Now I'm used to it,' she would say, 'now I like it. It's just what Jews do. I guess that's why I like it.'

We were always after her to tell us of her childhood back in the old country but she seemed to prefer to forget. Her only cherished memory was how people from the village would come to visit her mother sad and troubled, shoulders bent. Her mother Channa would take them into a small room off the kitchen, my young grandmother sitting quietly on the steps outside the door. When these visitors would come out of the room some time later, their back would be straight, their step light, their smiling faces glowing. Grandma's parents, well off in their old country, became poor immigrants in America, but at least they were safe. On Fridays, in my grandparents' lovely kitchen overlooking green woods and a small cool stream, we sat together preparing for the Sabbath. While the chicken was cooking and the walnuts were ground, while the liver was chopped and mixed with schmaltz, I used to polish Gramma's Shabbat candlesticks; I liked to watch my white rag turn greenish black as they began to gleam in the light streaming through the kitchen window.

Grandma Rose ('Reizl'), as a child in the shtetl by Kiev, and her sabbath candlesticks.

Grandma didn't mind my spiritual explorations outside of Judaism, but she didn't understand them, either. She would listen while I described experiences with shamans, with yogis, with meditation. Then she would shrug her famous shrug: 'I guess I'm more practical than all that,' she'd say, 'I don't really have any faith. I wish I did, it would be real nice, I think, easier, more satisfying. What can I do? I just don't.'

When she started to get a bit old, in her late eighties, not so busy with anything anymore (much to her dismay), she started taking private torah classes. 'I never knew most of this!' she told me over the phone, Cincinnati – India. She had been to synagogue almost every Sabbath for most of her life, but never really bothered to find out more. 'Do you know this stuff?' she asked, 'It is so *interesting!*' I asked her if she was feeling closer to God these days. 'Well, I'm not really sure what that means,' she answered, but in her voice was a blush, a glow.

Now she was sitting in her hospital bed, as tiny as a child, her nightgown looking hollow. She was so scared. I suddenly knew what we had to do. Locking my eyes with hers, I started singing 'Adon Olam' ('Master of the Universe', a central and beloved Jewish prayer). Grandma sang right back with me. Holding on like a brave survivor to the side of a sinking raft she sang, steady and clear, she knew the words much better than I did. When we finished we moved on to another, and another. She never stumbled. When we were done she had arrived on the shores of the other bank and her pale blue eyes reflected the turquoise lights of Ein Sof, the Eternal Infinity of the Holy One.

I started lighting Shabbat candles, after many years of absence, the year I fell in love with Catarina Da Orta, the year Grandma Rose forgot her name. I have a childhood photo of Reizel, (Rose, Grandma, may her memory be a blessing) over the wooden pedestal where her candlesticks gleam and shine. If I had a picture of Catarina, Channa Rachel (may her memory be a blessing), I would hang it there as well. When I light my candles on Sabbath Eve, the waves of the Arabian Ocean crashing on the shore outside my window, we are three sisters together, two in Gan Eden, one still here.

A special bond with Goa

Sucheta Potnis

Sucheta Potnis has been writing all her life, which is not to say that she has been published widely. In between, there have been marriages, children, a career in travelling, moving from Bombay to Goa, spending time playing with dogs, eating, drinking, bird-watching and thus generally making the most of her life.

June 10ᵗʰ 1959. Royal Nederland Navy's

Martin Mariner VP 306 took off from Ceylon to Karachi, from where it would leave once again for Holland, its final destination. In Ceylon, during the preparations for take off, it was noticed that the starboard engine was losing oil. The aircraft crew which included experienced engineers, dismantled the pistons, drained the oil and then tried it again. This time, the starboard engine started normally and no further problem was ob-

ALL PHOTOS COURTESY RICHARD GABELAR

served, so the aircraft was cleared to take off to Karachi.

The recorded log of communication between the aircraft and air traffic control at Madras and Colombo showed that all went to plan for a few hours. Then came the request from the aircraft; their starboard engine had shut off and they were low on fuel. They asked permission to land at Goa as an emergency.

The aircraft was given permission and they started their approach to the Dabolim airport in Goa. On board, the crew prepared for an emergency landing. With one engine out of commission they knew that it would be a bumpy landing, at the very least.

On 10th June, 1959, Goa had typical pre-monsoon weather with overcast skies and gentle wind with fairly good visibility. The Martin Mariner came in, losing height maybe a bit too quickly, listing a bit with one engine out. The pilot fought with the controls to steady the craft as it entered the periphery of the Dabolim airport.

Maybe just a foot could have made the difference – but the undercarriage of the aircraft brushed against the top of the boundary wall of the airport. The impact, although not great, was enough to shear away the lowered undercarriage of the ailing aircraft. Stumbling and out of control, the aircraft dragged along the tarmac, finally ground to a halt and burst into flames. The explosion was loud enough to be heard in the nearby town of Vasco.

The support services, the ambulance, the fire tender and airport personnel rushed to the burning plane, but nothing helped as fierce flames kept them at bay. Yet the rescuers managed to pull out some of the crew members.

At home in Holland, on that Wednesday, unbeknownst to them, the lives of eight families would change forever.

In Holland, schools have a holiday on Wednesdays, so the children have a free day. Special television programs for children are aired and it is a joyous day. Six year old Richard Gabeler came back home after play-

ing with his friends, happy and tired. In the living room sat a stranger in full Naval uniform and his mother was crying with her head bowed. Little Richard heard that his father had died in a far away place.

'I didn't know what died meant. I knew my father was away a lot, but that he always came back. And he always had some exciting gift for me from one of the far away places he had been to...'

It would take little Richard many weeks and much growing up to realise that his father was gone forever this time.

As Richard grew up he found out as much about his father as he could. And indeed, his father, Constantijn Nicolaas Gabeler, had been a highly decorated naval man. Having served in WW2, Richard's father had been part of many bombing missions against German targets in Normandy, and in Germany itself over Bremen and Hamburg. For this, he was one of the few pilots awarded the 'Flying Medal'.

Susanne Van Der Velden hummed to herself as she came back from work. She had every reason to be happy. Her fiancé, Manfred was due to return home from his overseas posting after a long time and the wedding was just a few weeks away. It would be a summer wedding. Since Manfred had been away, Susanne was the one who was looking after most of the wedding arrangements; the church, the music, the bridesmaids, her dress!

Then the phone rang – her mother in law to be. Mrs Baarspul generally called at this time to chat some more about the wedding. The two women had become close, more like friends than mother-in-law and daughter in law. Now, with Manfred's arrival so near, it would be an exciting chat.

'Hello Mum...' Susanne trilled and then paused; the voice on the other end was almost unrecognisable, anguished and broken – 'Manfred... Manfred's plane crashed'.

Susanne Van Der Velden never got married, for her, Manfred was the chosen one. If she couldn't marry him, she wouldn't want to marry anyone else. Susanne remains an extraordinary person with strong beliefs and indomitable spirit. A couple of decades ago, she found solace in Sufism, that gentle, spiritual sect of Islam which expresses devotion to God through music and poetry.

★ ★ ★

My brother in law, Alfred Tuinman, was approached by the Netherlands Consulate in India to look into the matter of the eight graves at St Andrew's cemetery in Vasco. Despite the Clergy's help, the old Dutch graves were crumbling, the headstones fallen down over the years. It took Alfred weeks to get the graves in better shape. The area was cleaned of roots and debris. New headstones were made with engraved epitaphs and the surroundings beautified.

The Dutch Naval ships, HNLMS Amsterdam and HNLMS Van Gaalen, arrived in Mormugao Port for the occasion. Relatives of the eight Dutch naval soldiers who died in the crash in 1959 were taken by a special flight from Holland to Goa.

Then, on 28th April 1997, a sombre but elegant ceremony saw the consecration of the graves at St Andrew's cemetery. For many relatives,

it was the first time that they were at the site where their family member had been buried.

A mass was celebrated by the Parish priest of the St Andrew's church and followed by a speech by the Dutch pastor. 'How the tragedy of Tenth June 1959 affected your life! Suddenly you're a widow; suddenly you have no father, no son, no brother! Let's hope being here today, at the graves of your dearest, you will find closure.'

Like Susanne's Van Der Velden favourite Sufi poetry tells us:

Mourn not the death of your beloved
Don't call back the traveller,
Who is on the journey to his goal,
For you know what he seeketh.
You are on the earth,
But he is now in heaven.
(Hazrat Inayat Khan)

A full ceremonial military funeral followed.

There are many reasons why people come to Goa. Even holiday

makers look for different things – rest, relaxation, sun, sea, culture and nature to name but a few.

When I met the families of the dead Dutch soldiers though, I felt their reasons for visiting Goa were unique. The fact that their nearest ones are buried in Goa has made this land a very special place for them. They have a special bond with Goa.

It was a special feeling with which we showed them Goa; the simple pleasure of walking through a spice plantation, the flight of a kingfisher on the river, a temple bell ringing at sunset and the distinct 'whoosh' as a dolphin surfaces from the deep waters.

At the end of their stay, one of the ladies said, 'If their plane had to go down somewhere, we are so thankful it happened in Goa.'

Note – This is a long story, full of courage, despair and heartbreak. I have tried to piece it together from the stories of some of the relatives and documents and photographs they so generously shared with me. Any omissions and mistakes are clearly mine.

Blood

Himanshu Burte

Himanshu Burte has finally accepted that he will keep moving across homes, disciplinary and real. Having practised architecture in an earlier life, he now writes full-time, obsessed with humans and the spaces they inhabit.

It was past one, and the bustle of the old
market street was dying down for the afternoon. Ambardekar Store looked
empty in spite of all the people and things that were there as always.
Because of the bright sunlight outside, it took everybody a moment longer
to wake up to the blood on the boy's clothes as he walked into the store
looking lost and disoriented. He must have been twelve or thirteen.
Savitribai noticed the blood on the front of his shirt only when he wandered well into the cool, dark and narrow depth of the shop and stopped
near her chair just under the tubelight. She looked up with the sober
alarm of those who have lived long and saw that it came from the wound
on his temple.

'*Arre!* What happened?' she asked in Marathi, looking at the boy
and back at the siesta bound street that had delivered him, as she began
easing out of her chair with the slow urgency her arthritis dictated.
Sambhaji, her son, and Ravindra, his assistant, moved out from behind
the counter at the same time.

'What happened?' Sambhaji asked coming around, his distant public
manner tinged with concern. He motioned Ravindra to fetch water as
he spoke. Ravindra opened a folding stool for the boy to sit, and then
moved away.

Still dazed, the boy sat down silently, looking around slowly at the
people his arrival seemed to have dislodged from different perches and

corners. He shrank a bit as they gathered around. Ravindra returned. The boy quenched his thirst, clutching the glass as though it held more than just water. As he finished, he found a rough, fat, wrinkled hand sitting lightly on his shoulder. He looked up and saw an old man with an open face and a receding mop of white hair above kind eyes. Laljibhai's voice was gentle as he asked in Marathi:

'Are you feeling better now, *beta?*'

The boy nodded. So he understood Marathi.

Savitribai, not yet out of her chair, turned to Anasuya, Sambhaji's wife who had come in with the lunch box for the family. Unlike the other shops, Ambardekar Store remained open through the afternoon. Sambhaji was suddenly glad that his eight year old son, Sandesh, was away at school.

'Shouldn't someone call the doctor?' asked Savitribai.

'I will go get him,' said the other shop assistant, who had remained steadfastly behind the other counter so far. Grey haired Mahadu, forever the hardworking 'boy', put on his slippers and hastened out into the blazing street.

Sambhaji turned to Laljibhai and asked softly, 'Do you think this will be a police case?'

'Looks like it,' said Laljibhai after a moment of thought. He turned again to the boy.

'What happened, *beta,* how did you get hurt? Did you have an accident? Did someone hurt you?'

The boy looked away into the street and did not speak. Then, he turned towards Savitribai and started crying into his shirt.

'Where are your parents, child?' Anasuya spoke for the first time, as if from the shadows.

'I don't know,' said the boy through his low whimpering.

Just then two or three men walked loudly past the shop, their rough chatter and the *thok! thok!* of their sticks ringing strangely through the emptiness of the street outside. More sounds, and some more men followed, but this time someone banged a stick on the small signboard of the shop propped up by the sidewalk and drew laughter from his companions.

Sambhaji walked quickly towards the open entrance of the shop and peered at the menacing backs of the loud strangers. Who were these people? A series of shouts followed further down the street from where the strangers had come.

It took him a moment to figure it out. He had never seen anything like it, after all. But he recognised the signs of what was coming from twenty years of reading and watching the news. A sense of weariness momentarily overcame him. Could it happen here? The very next moment, he had swiftly removed the signboard from the sidewalk, turned the pivoted racks displaying everything from shampoo satchets to chewing gum into the shop and begun pulling down the rolling shutter.

By this time Ravindra had already joined him at the rolling shutter and they both pushed the impossibly heavy cooler by the fraction of an inch required to let the shutter come all the way down.

'What's up?' Ravindra asked as they moved quickly.

'Trouble,' said Sambhaji.

'Sambhaji, what's happening?' called out Savitribai, worried at the unexpected flurry of activity. Meanwhile Laljibhai and Anasuya too had rushed out. As Anasuya picked up the flyers and loose packets that had slipped off the rack, Laljibhai looked back down the street where the shouting was building up in the distance. The contentment of a life spent well elsewhere in this same bazaar left his face. So he would see *this* now?

As everyone backed into the shop, Sambhaji pulled the shutter down, slipped the Godrej lock into its socket and turned the key. He turned to Ravindra and said, 'Ravi, call the doctor and tell him and Mahadu to lock up and get home fast. And then call Sandesh's school to tell them too, so we can pick him up early on the way home.'

Savitribai was intensely agitated now. 'What is happening? Will someone tell me?'

'There is trouble coming up the street, *aai*, we need to go home quickly.'

'What? And what about this boy?' she said, shocked.

The boy had been watching all the activity with growing fear. Anasuya was by his side already and holding his hand. Sandesh looked at her and at the boy. He knew the boy knew, perhaps better than Sandesh would ever know, what the storm on the street would bring.

'*Beta*, come let's go home.' So saying, they all trooped out the back door, each with a quick bow and prayer to the decorated image of the god in whose name blood would be spilt today.

Aniruddha Sen Gupta, *'Home produce', Panjim market, Goa, 2011*

Granny's Goa

Veena Gomes-Patwardhan

Veena Gomes-Patwardhan once lived amidst test tubes and petri-dishes.
Now whenever she can tear herself away from her computer, and when
she isn't driving her grown-up sons nuts doling out unasked-for advice, she
indulges in research and development in the kitchen.

It was a sultry evening in Bombay, sometime

in the 1960s. On the way home from school I had walked into my maternal grandmother's house, to find her in a foul mood. Usually, Granny's little kitchen reverberated with the cheerful hum of old melodies. But that day, she was muttering to herself, punching the chapati dough with undisguised ferocity. From the other room, I could hear sounds resembling a muted radio commentary. That was my grandpa, Militao Furtado, seated at the dining table, reading Ian Fleming's *Dr. No* – aloud! Grandpa had a habit of putting his finger below every word as he read line after line and page after page of any book… always aloud. Sometimes, he went back a few lines to read a sentence one more time to understand it better. Grandpa was crazy about books. No matter if they were penned by writers as different as Edgar Wallace, Zane Grey or A. J. Cronin, he devoured them all. Always immersed in his books, his hold on the real world was, to put it mildly, not very firm. But it was not just Grandpa's reading habits, almost everything about the man annoyed Granny.

That evening, sensing her fury, I asked, 'What's wrong, Granny?'

Jabbing a floury finger in the direction of Grandpa's voice, she retorted, 'Can you hear that droning? It's driving me crazy!'

'You're always angry with Grandpa,' I said, in the poor man's defence. 'Didn't you like him when you married him?'

'There was no question of not liking him,' she snapped.

'You mean you *had* to marry him?' was my horrified reaction.

'Well, no…' she conceded after a brief pause. 'I knew him as a distant relative and my parents had approved of him.'

She knocked the dough around some more and went on, 'But he was much older than me.' And for good measure she added, 'I used to call him Uncle.'

Uncle? This was weird. 'What do you mean you used to call him Uncle?' I asked.

'Well, when we got married, I was just 15. He was 30.'

Granny was just fifteen when she got married? I'll still be in school at fifteen, I thought to myself, speechless with disbelief.

★ ★ ★

Later, when Granny was her usual calm self again, she explained that in those days in Goa, brides were often still in puberty, while grooms were much older. There was no courtship, no getting to know each other before marriage, all that came later. And so, Granny had discovered Grandpa's little eccentricities only *after* they got married. Beforehand she only knew that he was of sound character and worked as a clerk in the British India Steamship Company in Bombay. Job openings being extremely few in Goa back then, many Goans found employment as manual workers or musicians in British India. A few like my Grandpa found white collar jobs. Granny recalled how one moment she was a surrogate mother to her siblings when their Mum was away tending to crops in their fields, and the next a child bride and young mother with kids of her own. However, she had to stay put in Goa till her first two children were born and joined Grandpa in Bombay only after he moved out of the village club into rented accommodation where they could all live together as a family.

Opportunities for conversations like this with Granny were many since she, as also most of my friends, lived in the building opposite my own. Located on a busy street, it had just a tiny compound at the back.

Granny's house.

So we kids made the wide corridors on each of the building's floors our playground instead, leaping agilely over banisters and zipping up and down the staircases much like Spiderman. Almost every evening, after playing with my friends I would pop in to see Granny. We would chitchat and laugh and sing and whenever she was less busy, she would reminisce about life in Goa. Stories of the Goa of yore were the ones I liked best. While Granny delved into the past, I would hang on to every word of hers, peeping wide-eyed into the window she threw open to a fascinatingly different world – to the time of simple living.

Christened Maria Santana Afonso, Granny was born in Betalbatim, Goa, in 1910, the same year a revolution overthrew the monarchy in Portugal, leading to the homeland of Goa's colonial rulers becoming a republic. In the decade that followed, several other significant events also occurred across the world, but little Maria and most ordinary Goans were oblivious to them.

In 1911, King George V of England and his consort Queen Mary arrived in Bombay on a historic visit following which the city's most famous monument, the Gateway of India, was erected to commemorate the occasion. On her maiden voyage across the Atlantic in April 1912, the 'unsinkable' Titanic struck a giant iceberg and sank like a stone resulting in more than 1500 watery deaths. In 1914, the First World War broke out and raged across Europe for the next four years, snuffing out the lives of millions. In 1915, a young lawyer, Mohandas Karamchand Gandhi, fired by nationalistic zeal, returned to India from South Africa, and a new chapter opened in the country's freedom struggle. The 20th century teens were indeed a mix of the best and the worst of times. But in Granny's Goa, life for the common man went on unperturbed by world events, whether exciting, catastrophic or otherwise.

Back then in Goa, people lived life in a different lane. They worked hard, rested well, came together to celebrate their feasts, shared their joys and sorrows with each other, and kept the spirit of community alive. On the way home from their fields or shops, men stopped at tavernas to swill a peg or two of *copachem* (locally brewed feni) before proceeding home for their mid-day meal or dinner. At such times, they talked about what was happening in each other's world and also kept abreast of the latest news. Such as – Pedro's wife having delivered a baby, or Antonette's daughter's impending wedding to a boy from Africa, or about Manuel's son having gone off to Bombay to study medicine. But mostly, talk would revolve around job prospects outside Goa or employment opportunities on the P&O passenger liners. Life was hard but the people were happy; at least that's what Granny always said during our many chats.

One evening, I popped into Granny's house, dishevelled and panting after an energetic round of '*Chor Police*', and found her pottering around in the kitchen getting the evening meal ready. Relieved to see me, Granny quickly sent me off to the bakery down the street. I was back in a flash, with oven-fresh loaves swathed in a scrap of newspaper.

'This bread smells so good,' I said.

'Yes,' said Granny. 'Reminds me of my childhood days in Goa. Did you know my father used to run a bakery?'

'A bakery? You never told me about this before!' I exclaimed, intrigued by this bit of news.

Curiosity flared up inside me and like our cat in Goa, who I had often watched crouching hopefully near the dining table waiting for fish bones to be thrown her way when meals were served, I waited with bated breath for Granny to begin her story. Although in the middle of preparing dinner, Granny put her work aside and proceeded to take me on a walk through family history.

A dashing young man with an adventurous streak, Granny's Dad, Marcelino Afonso, was unwilling to eke out a living from farming. He was keen to do something different, like run an enterprise of his own.

At that time, as now, bakers did brisk business. After all, bread was an indispensable commodity for everyone in Goa. But Salcete, the district in which Betalbatim was located, had a surfeit of bakeries. By a stroke of good luck, Marcelino heard about someone looking for a partner to run a bakery in Caranzalem, Panjim. This meant running a business far away from home, but he took the plunge. While the workers remained the same, Marcelino and his partner took turns in running the bakery, for four months at a time. The arrangement worked beautifully. Business was good and soon the bakery gained a reputation for the superb quality of its *unddes, bols, polis, kankonns* (different types of bread) and cakes. The two bakers joined their vendors in supplying bread to the surrounding wards and even to the Governor's Bungalow – the Cabo Palace (today's Raj Bhavan).

In 1908, Marcelino took a bride, Doroteia. The couple produced four offspring – Maria Santana, the eldest, followed by another daughter Paciencia, and two sons Pedro and Valerio. In the early years, when it was Marcelino's turn to run the bakery, he and Doroteia would pack their belongings and leave for Caranzalem, kids in tow, by whatever means of transport they could find. At that time, public transport consisted of the tiny Portuguese-run buses called *caminhões*. But they ran after long intervals and only along certain routes; so people often had to walk long distances to board them. However, private transport could be arranged by way of horse or oxen-drawn carriages.

Granny and her siblings always enjoyed journeying to Caranzalem and back, though it probably wasn't much fun for their parents who had to pack and carry the luggage, sometimes all the way to their boarding point, while simultaneously keeping an eye on their brood. Besides, the route also entailed a boat ride across the river Zuari from Cortalim to Agassaim.

In Caranzalem, the living quarters were behind the bakery. So every morning, Granny woke up to delicious aromas from the wood-fired oven. There were no electric mixers, no fancy gadgets, everything was hand-made and everything depended on the baker's skill. Once the loaves came out of the oven, plump and golden, they were arranged in baskets lined with a clean cloth, ready for sale. Soon they would grace the breakfast tables of the people in the vicinity. Granny's brothers, Pedro and Valerio, loved to help sell the bread each morning. They had fun doing the rounds, balancing the big bread-basket on their heads and jingling the bells on the vendor's staff they had to carry for announcing their arrival.

In 1916, before their last child was born, Marcelino bought some land at Betalbatim to build a house of his own. Just the bare walls of the house had been constructed when Goa was lashed by unseasonal rains. Terrified that the unprotected walls of her new house would come tumbling down, Doroteia prayed fervently to God and promised to build a cross in front of her new dwelling in gratitude if He protected it.

Marcelino and Doroteia's house and the cross they erected are both standing till today. The house doesn't have a very imposing foundation; but in the front, a long balcony runs along its width and its timber roof has a beautiful reverse gable in the centre. For me, it's the prettiest house in all of Betalbatim. These days, people driving by often slow down for a closer look. As for the cross, it now has a little shrine built around it. Bedecked with flowers and illuminated during the novena to the Holy Cross each year in May, the neighbours join the present generation of Afonsos here in thanksgiving. The bakery at Caranzalem also still exists, though the ownership has now changed hands.

Once the children started going to school, Marcelino made the trips to Caranzalem alone. At harvesting time the older Afonso children, like others in the village, helped their parents in the fields. Though not expected to do much, the children loved joining the grown-ups in tasks such as filling the baskets with the threshed paddy, stripping ruby red chillies off their shrubs, yanking onion bulbs out of the ground, or shaking the mud off uprooted sweet potatoes. Even as he attended to his own tasks, Marcelino kept an eye on the kids, yelling warnings now and then and reminding them to keep out of the way of the shovels and sickles. I could envision how much better and more fun this hands-on education was in Granny's days, compared to what I had to learn from the pages of boring school text books.

By sundown the children would be asked to run off home and have a wash. Unimaginable today, but back then, they had no running water. So they had to wash their mud-caked bodies at the family well, squealing with delight as they upturned pots of the manually drawn refreshingly cool water over their heads.

Every afternoon, after cooking lunch, Doroteia threw a couple of onions, potatoes, and sweet potatoes into the dying embers of the kitchen hearth. These cooked to perfection in the hot ash and were ready for the children to gorge on when they returned from play or from school. Sometimes she prepared *goddxem* out of kidney beans, rice and jaggery, or *nachni* gruel. These were healthy treats for the children. Come to think of it, folks at that time didn't have to watch what they ate or go on diets. Everything they ate seemed good for them. Granny told me that later on she too had adopted her Mum's strategies for stretching meagre resources and keeping her kids well fed.

★ ★ ★

I remember another evening when I dropped in at Granny's place as usual and found her in her favourite chair which she had moved closer to the balcony to catch the last of the fading daylight. She was chuckling over the comic strip 'Bringing up Father' in the Free Press Journal. Leaning over her shoulder, I tried to see what the tussle between Jiggs and Maggie was about that day. As usual, the fight seemed to have ended with a rolling pin flying in poor Jiggs's direction! I couldn't help suppressing a smile for my Dad always joked about my Mum's parents being perfect replicas of Maggie and Jiggs, mainly because of their many silly tiffs. But unlike Maggie, Granny was a sensible, self-made woman. On an impulse, I whispered 'Good evening, Granny' into her ear, causing her to reach behind, and rap me playfully on the shoulder for creeping up on her.

Noticing Grandpa was nowhere in sight, I pointed to his neat pile of books on the dining table.

'Where's Grandpa?'

'God knows. Burying his head into one newspaper after the other at the Irani restaurant downstairs most probably,' said Granny frowning.

I couldn't blame her for that irritated comment. Grandpa's voracious appetite for the printed word was known to the whole family.

'Grandpa's just a bit of a dreamer,' I said trying to calm Granny down. 'He's not all that bad.'

'I know,' she said with a resigned sigh. 'There are worse husbands...'

That's how Granny was – level-headed and down-to-earth. Looking back, I can now see how Granny's remarkable pragmatism had helped her shoulder adult responsibilities at a very tender age in Goa and had then sustained her through highs and lows in later life.

Today sadly Granny is no more, but the tête-à-têtes with her have stayed with me as childhood milestones. Though I didn't know it then, I was discovering parts of my heritage, and carefully stashing them away like treasures in my memory. Looking ahead, I wonder what I'll tell my own grandchildren someday. What thoughts and experiences will I share with them? Today, the world is changing so fast. It's impossible to predict how it will be even a decade from now. People may do things differently; perhaps even fruits and flowers may grow differently.

So I wonder how far back in time I'll take them when my grand-children say, 'Granny, tell us about the old days.' Maybe I'll start with, 'When I was little, there was no TV....' In all probability, this bombshell alone will squeeze gasps of horror out of their little throats, like the ones we used to hear in darkened cinema halls during Alfred Hitchcock films.

Anthony Vaz

Amitav Ghosh

Amitav Ghosh is one of India's best-known writers. He divides his time between Kolkata, Goa and Brooklyn.

I have long been fascinated by nautical

dictionaries, especially those that relate to Asian seafarers (or 'lascars' as they were once known). Elsewhere I have written at some length about Lieutenant Thomas Roebuck's magisterial lexicon of the Laskari language (*An English And Hindostanee Naval Dictionary*), which was first published in Calcutta in 1811: 'Born in 1781, Roebuck was a skilled linguist, who had served a rigorous apprenticeship under the famous John Borthwick Gilchrist, author of the first major Hindi-English dictionary. From 1806 to 1809 Roebuck was in Edinburgh assisting Gilchrist to prepare his lexicon. After that, while traveling to Calcutta on the Hon'ble Company Ship *Larkins*, Roebuck passed his time by compiling his Naval Dictionary ... Roebuck did not long survive the publication of his dictionary, dying of a fever in Calcutta at the age of 38. But he did live to see the proof of his work's usefulness, for in 1813, two years after its first publication, his Dictionary was reprinted by the East India Company's booksellers in London. In 1882 it was revised and reissued by a missionary called George Small, under the title *A Laskari Dictionary Or Anglo-Indian Vocabulary Of Nautical Terms And Phrases In English And Hindustani*.[1] Under that name it continued to circulate well into the 20th century.'[2]

Roebuck's was not the only dictionary of this kind in circulation in the 19th and early 20th centuries. There were a few others, including one by a Goan (or possibly East Indian) seaman called Anthony Vaz.

Vaz was by profession a master sailmaker ('silmagoor' in Laskari), employed in the government dockyard in Bombay in the 1870s. But he was also, evidently, a dedicated wordsmith for in 1879 he published a fine compendium called: *The Marine Officer's Hindustani Interpreter Containing A Vocabulary Of Nautical Terms, Directions For Masting, Rigging And Working Ship At Sea*, (Bombay Gazette Steam Press, Bombay, 1879).

The preface to this booklet is interesting enough to quote at some length. Vaz writes: 'Under the favourable auspices of commerce the number of ships visiting the several seaports of India has of late years greatly increased and shipowners, who confine their operations chiefly to this part of the world, have found it profitable to employ Indian crews on their vessels. Against the advantages offered by the employment of these men have to be weighed some petty inconveniences, one of which is felt in conveying orders in the native language with which ships officers are, in a majority of cases, unacquainted. This Book is an humble effort to help those who have not acquired a sufficient knowledge of the vernaculars, in giving the various orders to the seamen, incidental on board a ship.... In getting up the work I have drawn entirely upon my own resources, depending of the knowledge of seamanship acquired by rote during fourteen years service at sea and have therefore to crave the indulgence of the public for any shortcomings they may find therein.

'Hindustani is the language into which the sentences have been rendered – not literally, but as the natives are accustomed to hear the orders shouted out, in most cases in a contracted form, and the spelling is adopted on the same principle without regard to the Jonesian or any other system. The rendering into the vernacular is not Oordoo or the critical style spoken by the Mahomedans of Delhi or the Deccan Hyderabad, as such translation would be quite out of place on board a ship, from the inability of the men generally to comprehend that style. The technical names of Spars, Yards, the standing and running Rigging,

Gears, Sails and words that relate to the manoeuvring and working of ships at sea are all Arabic in their origin.'

There are several striking differences between Roebuck's diction-ary and Vaz's. The most important perhaps is that Roebuck was attempt-ing to make the case that 'Laskari' was, if not a language, then certainly a dialect in its own right, created out of the merging of many different languages – Arabic, Portuguese, English, Bengali, Malay, Malayalam, Tamil, Kachhi and so on (although a few Marathi words figure in his dictionary I cannot remember any specifically Konkani terms). But Vaz does not anywhere acknowledge or use the term 'Laskari' – even the word 'lascar' does not figure in his book. This is probably because this word had, by the late nineteenth century, acquired pejorative racial con-notations: as a seaman himself, Vaz would have been acutely aware of these connotations. Such indeed was the stigma attached to the word 'lascar' that it more or less fell out of usage after the Second World War.

Throughout his dictionary Vaz insists that the language of Indian seamen is Hindustani, except for the 'technical names' which, he asserts 'are all Arabic in their origin'. In point of fact this is not true at all: many of the words for the rigging, masts, sails etc. came from other languages, especially Portuguese. For example, the Laskari word for 'mizzen-sail' was *trikat* which comes from the Portuguese *traquete*. Similarly, *taliyamar*, the Laskari word for 'cutwater' came directly from the Portuguese *talhamar*. There are innumerable such examples.[3]

Vaz was not an etymologist of course, but even then it remains something of a puzzle that he should have been unaware of the Portu-guese influences on the nautical vocabulary of the Indian subcontinent.

Unlike Roebuck, Vaz was in the first instance, a seaman and one interesting aspect of his dictionary is that its organisation is dictated by practical, rather than lexical considerations. In effect the book is a com-pendium of the commands that are necessary to the operation of a sailship, and they are divided according to certain tasks: for example 'Launching

of the Ship', 'Making Sails When Fine Daylight'; 'Bracing Yards in Calm
When Wind Not Steady', 'Setting and Taking Studding Sails When Fine
Steady Breeze.'

The reader may be interested here to examine some of the commands and their glosses, so here are a few:

From 'Launching of the Ship':
- All hands clean clothes   – *sab admee saf*
  on board   *kupray payno*
- Cock well the anchor   – *lungur cock well karo*
- Take in the ballast   – *leelum layo*

From 'Setting Trying Sails and Spreading the Awnings':
- Clew up the royal, gallant – *stringee tubber, subber*
  sail and top sails, fore   *gabee agul pitchel*
  and aft
- All your clewline, buntline – *chop stringee buntline*
  and leechline close up   *seesee door cheekar*

From 'Bracing Yards About in Calm When Wind Not Steady'
- Square the main yard   – *yam burra purwan*
- Haul out the spanker   – *tan bar ghoosee*

From 'Setting and Taking in Studding Sails When Fine Steady Breeze'
- Topmen aloft   – *panjrawala oopur jao*
- Set the fore top gallant   – *hankar trinket subber*
  studding sail   *dustoor*

Today the English commands are no more comprehensible than
their translations. This is of course because every sailship was, in a sense,
a vast, floating dictionary, with thousands of named parts – every gasket,

leech and pin had its own name. With the vanishing of wind-powered merchant vessels, this entire apparatus (of words as well of things) has more or less disappeared from the face of the earth. This is precisely the value of books like Vaz's: they give us a glimpse of a way of life that is now extinct. It is very unfortunate that we do not have any direct testimonies of this way of life – but I am convinced that there are many yet undiscovered manuscripts languishing in Goan houses. Let us hope that they will soon come to light.

1. Roebuck, Capt. Thomas: *A Laskari Dictionary Or Anglo-Indian Vocabulary Of Nautical Terms And Phrases In English And Hindustani,* revised and corrected by George Small, W.H.Allen & Co., London, 1882.

2. This excerpt is from my article 'Of Fanas and Forecastles' which was published in the Economic and Political Weekly in 2008.

3. Cf. Soares, Anthony Xavier.: *Portuguese Vocables in Asiatic Languages from the Portuguese Original of M.S.R. Dalgado (translated into English with Notes, Additions and Comments),* Asian Educational Services, New Delhi & Madras, 1988, pp. 350 & 340.

Tsunami Simon

Damodar Mauzo
Translated from the Konkani
by **Xavier Cota**

*Born, bred and living in the not-so-quiet seaside village of Majorda in
South Goa, Damodar Mauzo was once termed by an anchor on Delhi
Doordarshan as an 'honorary Catholic' for his in-depth writings depicting
the Catholic lifestyle of Goa. He is mainly a writer of short fiction,
though his novels 'Karmelin' and 'Tsunami Simon' have also become
widely popular.*

*When Xavier Cota is not busy stirring his fellow villagers to protect their
coastal village of Betalbatim, he is engrossed in translating his friend
Damodar Mauzo's Konkani stories.*

But even ten days after Bula's Anniversary Mass,

Dulcin would just not let her go. Dulcin, who had turned silent with grief since Bula's death, had started opening up in the company of Marcelin. The sisters would talk on endlessly. 'What's that noise outside?' Marcelin got up first. Dulcin also rose to investigate the sound of running feet.

'What's going on, Caitu?' she asked Caetan who was running towards the sea.

'It seems that a dolphin's been caught in Santan's net!'

Dulcin remembered that some time ago, a female dolphin, nearly two-metres long, had been trapped in Gabru's net. Gabru had carefully released her into the creek, where all the fisher-folk kids from *Kharvyanvaddo* had a wonderful time playing with her. Even Bula had hitched a ride on the dolphin's back.

Everybody was making a beeline for the beach. What a mad rush! Santan was driving the people away in irritation. It appeared from his behaviour that he wanted the people to go away so that he could take the dolphin away and cut it up.

Dulcin went close to it. This one was smaller than the dolphin which had been caught in Gabru's net a couple of years ago. She hadn't been dragged up the shore yet. Whenever a wave washed up, she would flap around helplessly in an attempt to get away. The entreating eyes of the dolphin began to wrench at Dulcin's heart. The look was so familiar. It was Bula! The same guileless, trusting eyes.

'Is that a dolphin?' An Indian tourist was excitedly getting ready to click a photograph.

Santan was fuming. Shouting, 'Vassimbor, get lost! It is not dolphin. It is hiskadi. Now get out! Do not disturb,' he moved menacingly towards him. The poor tourist scampered away in fright.

The locals did not say anything. Everybody knew that the dolphin was a protected species under the law. In any case, a traditional fisherman would never kill a dolphin. Whenever one was caught, it would be released into the sea. After allowing the children to play with it for some time, Gabru too had released the dolphin into the sea. But today's youth had developed a taste for dolphin meat. They would often clandestinely kill and eat the creatures. Besides, the meat fetched a good price too.

'Arre Santan, you'd better release the dolphin into the sea. You may be reported.' Jaki, the elderly fisherman advised him quietly.

Santan snarled angrily, 'I'll whack anybody who opens his mouth! Does anyone dare? Go away all of you!' Turning back to Jaki, he said in a low voice but with a malevolent smile, 'Our minister will be very pleased. He loves this meat. You go along home. I'll take care of this.'

Santan had managed to obtain a subsidy and license for a motorised boat after begging and pleading with the minister. He now used it for fishing even during the breeding season when fishing was prohibited. It was well known that whenever he caught any protected fish and even turtles, he would promptly send some as a gift to the minister.

Dulcin caught Santan's words. She looked again at the dolphin. It was the same entreating look. The look of Bula. Whenever Bula did something wrong, Dulcin would say, 'You deserve a spanking!' and raise her hand. But on seeing Bula's pleading eyes and contrite voice, 'No Mai, I'll never do this again. Please don't beat me!' involuntarily her hand would be lowered. More than her voice, Bula's beseeching eyes evoked pity.

Dulcin looked at the eyes of the dolphin which, like a child's, were now filled with tears. 'Santan, for God's sake, please release her into the sea! Please, for the love of God!'

The sound of her tremulous voice and tear-filled eyes stunned everyone around. Santan who had opened his mouth to roar was left open-mouthed.

'Please Santan! Look at her eyes! Please!' Marcelin stepped forward. Putting her arms round her sister, she began to soothe her.

'Just look at her eyes, Marcelin. They are my Bula's eyes. Tell him! Tell him to let her go.' Dulcin broke into sobs.

The atmosphere at the beach had undergone a complete transformation. And at that very moment Gabru appeared.

Gabriel Baptista was a traditional fisherman, proud to belong to the fishing community and well-respected for his integrity. When Gabru stepped out, four of Santan's cronies surreptitiously drew back.

'Santan, you are a traditional fisherman. What are you doing with that dolphin?'

Santan did a quick mental calculation. If the incident got publicity, even his minister friend would not be able to save him.

'Who says I'm pulling her out of the water? Of course I'm going to release her into the sea.'

'So why are you waiting? Come on, man.'

Dulcin moved forward and hugged the dolphin, running both her hands all over her body and wiping her tear-filled eyes. The gratitude in the dolphin's eyes was palpable to everyone around.

The net was promptly raised and carried into the water. It was opened slowly and the dolphin gently lifted out and released into the open sea. The dolphin responded by turning around in a circle. She then gave a couple of graceful leaps before merging into the blueness of the sea.

Simon had reached the shore with his friends a short while back, after hearing about the dolphin. He'd watched everything with bated breath. His chest now swelled with pride and admiration for the way his parents had acted.

Excerpted from 'Tsunami Simon', the Konkani novel by Damodar Mauzo, published in 2009. The English translation by Xavier Cota will be published shortly.

Aniruddha Sen Gupta, 'Bringing in the catch', Siridao, Goa, 2008

Frederick Noronha, 'Boy with fish', Tivim, Goa, c. 2002

A childhood
spent in Africa

Tony de Sa

*Tony de Sa has tinkered for decades in the positions of teacher, supervisor
and headmaster at Sacred Heart, Parra, one of Goa's oldest English
medium schools. He is now in his second childhood, fooling around with
computers and Linux.*

Africa has always drawn people of other lands

to its bosom as a magnet draws nails to itself. Some came to Africa for the sake of exploration. Others came to seek adventure and fortune –big game, ivory, gold and diamonds. For yet others it was simply to earn their livelihoods. My father was one of those who were forced to make the perilous and uncertain journey to Africa for sheer economic reasons. It was thus that he found himself in Africa as a teenager, on the shores of the bleak salt marsh called Lake Magadi, working for the store at Magadi Soda Factory.

Africa was a land of opportunity and before long my father soon found employment with the Shell Company of East Africa. In the course of his work, he found himself being transferred to all parts of East Africa. He was posted at Eldoret, a small and rather primitive town then in the Rift Valley Province of Western Kenya.

When my mother was carrying for the fourth time, the arrival of the child was awaited with bated breath by all and particularly the three sisters who preceded this baby. According to Goan popular beliefs, a boy after three girls is termed a 'ticlo' and this is supposed to bring good fortune to the family. Many candles were lit, particularly to St. Anthony for the favour of a boy! Fortune surely smiled on the de Sa family when I was born. I was duly christened Anthony.

I was barely twenty two days old when my father got a transfer to another small town – this time to Moshi, Tanzania, which lies at the foothills of Mt. Kilimanjaro, the highest mountain in Africa. Moshi was where I grew up, one of the towns in Africa of which I have the fondest memories. My earliest memories of Moshi begin from 1954.

I did my primary studies at the Aga Khan School which was run by the Ismaili community. School there was fun and the learning experiences we had are engraved in my mind. A small Goan staff at school made our participation in dramas and cultural events a must. There were other teachers too from many different communities – ethnic Africans, Europeans, and Asians. Most were not trained, but worked wholeheartedly and made learning most interesting. I can hardly remember a time when we felt bored in school. Most of our days were filled with all kinds of activity. The most interesting subject of all was Art. Here we were given a variety of materials to play around with. We had clay moulding, plasticine, crayons, water colours, pencils, powder colours and the like. The syllabus was not so rigid and the teachers were given a free hand to teach their subject the way they liked. It was inevitable that we had to learn serious subjects like English, Math, Science, History, Geography and Kiswahili, nevertheless all the teachers made learning a pleasure. That is why till date, I have never set much score by training which is so all important in Goa. Training imparts communication skills and organised teaching skills but does not necessarily impart things like devotion and dedication and joy and enthusiasm for work.

When I was in the eighth standard, I was transferred to the Government Indian Secondary School, Moshi. Admission here was not smooth, simply because of a quirk of fate. Most of us had Portuguese passports. We were in that no man's land where we were neither Europeans nor Indians. Our ethnicity was plainly Indian. So it was with a great deal of persuasion and no little amount of subtle pressure that we were allowed in. For second language we were offered a choice of Gujarati or Urdu. We Goans were hopeless at both. However the authorities were considerate and started teaching us Hindi right from scratch.

Here also school was fun though the studies became more rigorous since we were being prepared for the Senior Cambridge exam. Gone were the days of fun in the class room since the teachers, mostly Indians from other states adopted a straightforward, no nonsense approach. However, there was compensation. There were games – hockey, football and in-door games, carrom and table tennis. We also had Scouting. Wow, the adventures we had! Camping with impromptu bed sheet tents, cooking and eating badly cooked meals, hiking and adventures – being hauled to the roof of the school by a rope, rope walking, building monkey bridges, trestles and watch towers. Dramatics were encouraged and we always managed to put up a Goan item of one sort or another for the school concert.

Our social life was again very rich. We were a small Goan community comprising of a handful of families. On Sundays, the seniors organised community picnics where every family contributed a dish. Many a house wife took great pride in presenting some novel dish, usually but not necessarily Goan in flavour. The picnic spots were always exotic and invariably close to rivers. Moshi had a choice of picnic spots – Marangu falls, high up on the slope to Mt. Kilimanjaro, Taveta Springs, Kibosho and Arusha Chini to name a few. Since my father was a Depot Manager at that time, it was always easy to arrange transportation. All he had to do was to persuade some merchant to loan us a lorry. The merchants usually obliged. So my father had the privilege of sitting in the cabin along with a couple of other seniors. The rest had to lump it at the back. Once we reached the spot, there were games, cards, singing and of course the food. We children always went home very reluctantly. When there were no picnics, there were indoor games and tombola at the club. Since the Gujaratis, Sikhs and Ismailis outnumbered the small Goan community, we always had a lot of friends from other communities. Some of us, including myself could fluently speak Gujarati, the most widely spoken language of the Asian community.

The Government had allotted plots of land to each community and we were fortunate to have a nice though hilly plot. It had a small wooden structure which was later replaced by a pucca cement structure further up the hill. It was here that I had my first sneak drive in a car. We children were fond of holding the steering wheel when elders were driving. I once held the steering of my school bus (a seven tonner Austin), while the African driver, Saidi, happily gunned the bus. Since my father didn't own a car, I pestered an 'uncle' to let me drive his Morris Minor. I worried him so much, preying on his kind nature that he tossed the keys to me and said, 'Go and kill yourself.' I managed to take two rounds of the small ground before stalling the car.

Our club was called the Goan Association and since the Goans there, to a man, were Catholics, we always thought that Goans were only Catholics. The unexpected descended upon us in the form of Molu Dessai, a Hindu gentleman from Cuncolim, Goa. He was initially barred from entering the club premises. After much heated debate, better counsel prevailed and he was finally admitted. It was then that it finally dawned upon us that there could be Hindu or Muslim Goans too.

I was about to start the new term in standard IX when fate played a card that would change the lives of my family members. For starters, My father who was advancing in age, and slaving away at his second job after having retired from Shell, was told that his services would not be required as the company had to employ a certain number of ethnic Africans because 'Uhuru' (Independence) was imminent and nationalism and national priorities were the order of the day. This was a disaster of pretty big magnitude as we were a large family and my father was the main bread winner; my eldest sister worked for a pittance in a private company. With a certain amount of desperation, my father called a family council meeting to order.

In our family, the system was that discussions were 'open-house' and everyone in the family took part freely except for times when matters not to be heard by children were discussed. In this discussion, while my brother and I remained mute spectators, my parents and my eldest sister thrashed out the alternatives. My father received a meager pension. His continued employment meant survival for the family. My eldest sister was quite independent. But the rest of us needed caring for, as for the most part we were students. My father then took himself off to Dar es Salaam, the national capital, where my second sister and her husband lived. My father managed to get a temporary job in a government department and sent for the rest of us. So we moved ourselves, bags and baggage to Dar es Salaam. For me, the journey to Dar es Salaam was again another experience. A friend of the family was driving down to Dar in his brand new Peugeot 403 and some of us were offered a lift. My mother, my brother and I made it to Dar by car. On the way, the driver managed to have a minor accident which made the trip all the more exciting.

Moshi paled in comparison to Dar. Moshi was fun, yes, but Dar opened new vistas. I was enrolled in a convent school run by an order of Swiss nuns. Here we had a mix of students from every community – Goan, Indian, European, African, a smattering of Chinese, Seychelloise and Mauritians. Quite a cosmopolitan mix I should say. The classes were interesting except for French which I had never learnt. A few misfits like me were sent to the Principal. Since most of us were from upcountry or different schools, we had never studied French. After a long lecture where we tried to explain the reasons for our handicap, she finally relented and allowed us to take Kiswahili the national language, which most of us were familiar with.

One of the co-curricular activities here was Scouting. I remember being taken to Bagamoyo creek to be taught swimming. Fr. Birch, popularly known as 'Pop Birch' simply dumped us into slightly deep water and told us to sink or swim. I was fortunate because in Moshi, due to the many picnics near the rivers, I had learnt to swim. The down side of schooling at Dar was that I had to trudge to school and back from my house in the suburbs, sometimes twice. Again we had Goan teachers who lost no opportunity to complain to my sisters or my parents about my many transgressions whenever they met them at the Goan Institute or after mass.

The social life of the Goan community was centred round the Goan Institute. My family members were regular club goers and usually went there on a Sunday and on most week days. The GI was a unique building designed by a Goan architect, Anthony Almeida. The building itself was built in the form of the letter 'G' and there was an open air dance floor resembling the letter 'I'. From the air, it was supposed to look like GI. I never did check that out as we simply did not have the shillings to throw around for plane rides. The building was unique in that it had separate rooms for different activities – cards, billiards, smoking, bar, library and reading room. There was a largish hall, offices and rest rooms. Sundays were devoted to tombola with big prizes in cash. There were no picnics like we had in Moshi, but we had a lot of family outings to the beaches – Oyster Bay and Tanganyika Packers near Kolito Barracks.

As my father was very fond of fishing, we would go fishing at various places. Soon it became a fashion to angle at Slender Bridge while the tide was coming in and catch lady fish which were fairly easy to catch. We youngsters often sneaked off to the beaches without telling any adult. I would bunk school and catch fish at the Customs Jetty. This was accomplished by bribing the lady at the school gate and crossing the street to the customs jetty. This trick worked well until I was caught one day and made to go to the teacher's house after school in the afternoon and sit patiently while she taught me the lesson I had missed. My class teacher also informed my parents and I got a tanning.

Fate then played its second card. My father lost his job again as a result of Africanisation, a policy where all non ethnic persons were replaced by ethnic Africans. Because my father was of advanced age, all he could get after that were temporary jobs of three months duration. My father, who by then was fed up with jumping from job to job ('like a monkey,' in his words), decided to call it quits. The only alternative he had was to come home to Goa, like a wounded animal going back to its lair. The small pension would barely make ends meet, but would suffice, with some amount of sacrifice in Goa.

Since I would be repeating the term in Goa, it was decided that I should stop studying and do the running around preparatory to our departure by ship to Goa. This task thrust responsibility on my shoulders. I had to get the passports from the Indian High Commission because Goa was 'liberated' then and we became Indian Citizens. Our adults, having been brought up in a different tradition, mostly looked upon Indians as 'dirty', little realising that we ourselves were Indians I had a nasty experience with the Indian High Commission because the Punjabi clerk there was delaying our passport for flimsy reasons. Little did I realise that he wanted baksheesh. I got impatient and asked to see the High Commissioner. After some argument in which I must have been pretty rude, I told him, 'Is this what we were liberated for?' He came back with, 'In Punjab, little boys like you don't talk too much.' I told him that we were not in Punjab and that must have done the trick for he gave me the passport. I then had to get the Immigration stamp in case my father had to return sometime in the future, and the ticket, and go through no small amount of formalities at the bank.

But these exercises – bank work, dealing with public officials and carrying large sums of money gave me a new sense of responsibility and confidence. I was able to shoulder much of the responsibilities of our house in Goa later on. This was an excellent training exercise. And so the day dawned when we had to leave Africa for Goa and a new life. That's another story for another day.

The fever

José Lourenço

José Lourenço writes with his brain and his heart, using English for the former and Konkani for the latter. Since he doesn't know which is which, he is often guilty of bilingual intercourse.

When Somoni Desai felt that the heat in his

lower body was getting too much, he went to Doctor Shivram. The doctor tucked up his *puddvem* and peered at Somoni's tongue. He asked him to cough as he studied Somoni's balls and watched them rise and fall.

Then he stood him in the sunlight streaming through the window of oyster shells and stared at the floor.

'It's a fever,' he said. 'Your shadow has a fever.'

Somoni went home very saddened. As he walked home in the fading light, he did not look behind him. But before he went to bed, he looked at the dark form cast on the lime-washed walls by the oil lamp and felt that his shadow did look a bit swollen.

'Which shadow has the fever, doctor?' he asked Doctor Shivram the next morning. 'My day shadow or night shadow?'

Doctor Shivram peered at him angrily over the spectacles he was not wearing. 'Do I look like the kind of doctor who examines night shadows?' he asked in a huff. 'Go to that Doctor Balachandravelu down the street if you want to know those things.'

Somoni walked back home in the afternoon sun, worried about his shadow. It had shrunk now and he squatted on the road for a while and touched it. It felt warm and feverish indeed. He felt a pang of shame for not having taken good care of it and vowed to make things right. He walked home slowly, his stunted shadow shuffling forlornly behind him.

'Sit still and don't move,' his wife warned him before she began rubbing his shadow with warm coconut oil and neem leaves, as he sat in his verandah that late afternoon. She continued massaging it every hour as it lengthened, only ceasing when it faded away into the hazy shades of dusk. Somoni stood up, and stepping gingerly over the now slippery floor, went into his house. He bathed and then lay in bed for the rest of the day.

'Don't go to the shop,' she warned him the next morning. 'The smell of tamarind and onion will make the fever worse.'

The *gaddekar* came by that evening and whipped his shadow with the branches of the *jagom* tree. As he took a break to light his bidi, Somoni asked him, 'This *zaddnim* is done mostly for mad dog bites, isn't it?'

'Mad dogs, snakes and shadows,' said the *gaddekar* as he blew smoke into his own crotch. He was not happy with the three rupees that Somoni's wife gave him and as he left he said, 'That mango tree there may not bear fruit next year.'

On the fourth morning, Somoni rose to go to his shop. He gently walked his shadow behind him all the way from his house to the bazaar. He steered it clear of potholes and made it walk on the grass as far as possible. At one point he stopped to check its temperature and was pleased to see that it had cooled down.

He sat at the cracked wooden counter of his shop in the face of the morning sunshine that soon framed the faces of his regular customers. He knew his shadow was mingling with those of the dusty black cupboard and the kerosene drum and the crates of soft drink bottles that lay at the back of the shop. Somoni didn't mind.

He even paused under a gulmohur tree on the way home to let his shadow race off and get lost in the shade of the branches, to play *apa-lipa* with the rays of light streaming through the leaves. When he stood up and walked back home, it obediently followed him, nipping along, between and around his legs like a mischievous dog.

'The fever is almost gone,' said Doctor Shivram with his ear to the floor. 'But there is still a weakness. Feed it cunji thrice a day.'

On the way home, Somoni remembered ex-Prime Minister Morarji Desai and paused to relieve himself, tracing wide arcs of urine to fully irrigate the form on the ground.

'Why don't you sleep on my bed at night?' he asked his wife when she brought him his milk for the night.

She sat on the bed next to him and they stared at their shadows on the lime-washed walls for a long while.

'After Babulo…after the baby went, I cannot…' she finally said with a crack in her voice.

Somoni saw her shadow small and forlorn on the lime-washed wall and wished his shadow would reach out and comfort hers. But all four of them sat still for a silent and heavy moment until the monsoon wind blew in from Canacona in the south, up to Balli and Fatorpa and their little mud walled house and whispered softly through their window, making the flame of the oil lamp - which was made of an empty cough syrup bottle - quiver and dance.

Somoni looked at their shadows swaying to the flicker of the lamp and said, 'See how they are dancing, Parvati!'

Parvati giggled and then blushed. Somoni also blushed as he watched his shadow's hand rest on her shoulder. He looked away from the wall in embarrassment as their shadows embraced and became one dark, irregular jackfruit shape.

Deep into the night the wind fell silent and the flame of the lamp stood as still and erect as a finger of Shiva, but the shadows on the wall continued to rise and fall, sometimes gently and sometimes feverishly.

Feast

Rosalyn D'Mello

Surrogate daughter of Henry Miller and Anais Nin, Rosalyn D'Mello lives life like a lens, swallowing images, and recognizing what makes them sublime before putting the lens over her readers' eyes. Her words, like LSD, attempt to make reality seem fantastic.

For you the choicest meat: drumsticks, plump
ones, from Republic of Chicken. I washed them, made incisions at the
intersections between flesh and flesh, and with my bare fingers, rubbed
the marinade so it would seep deep down into the bones. It's an old
Goan recipe, African in origin. We call it Cafreal.

*Grind six devious-green chillies with an inch-long piece of both cinna-
mon and ginger, ten fat cloves of garlic, about a tablespoon each of coriander,
cumin, and peppercorn seeds and four-to-five pieces of clove and cardamom.
Add vinegar. Palm vinegar. The kind that evolves only when toddy is left to
meditate in a clean container for at least 21 days. To this add a coarsely chopped
onion, and a touch of salt. Grind until you can no longer hear the cinnamon
stick grating against the walls of the mixer, until the onion gives up its soul,
until the ginger and the garlic mingle into each other and together enter the
community of ground spices. Grind until you are left with a thick, pulpy, rich
green paste and the scent of a Goan kitchen.*

I enmeshed the legs with the marinade and had a sip of red wine.
An inconsequential detail, I understand, but red wine does things to me,
mixes with my blood, flows through secret pathways in my brain until I
relent…

For you, no skimping on ingredients, no scrimping with cheese.

Crumbled bits of feta sit alone in a bowl. I split a dozen cherry tomatoes into two. They contrast with the crisp white of the goat cheese. I tear some iceberg lettuce, tear it like a writer destroying his masterpiece; calculatingly, so it can be re-constructed in the event of regret. Olives. Sliced into oblong little pieces, so little they will surprise your tongue when you half-bite into them. The same with jalapenos. And long slivers of sun-dried tomato all bathed in extra virgin olive oil. The feta is no longer alone. A drizzle of balsamic, a sprinkling of fresh basil. I toss all the ingredients and they jostle for space, they nudge and tug, shuffle and hug, and sigh.

I transport the half prepared meal from my kitchen to yours, a transfusion of sorts, and I stop on the way to buy some potatoes, just in case, and a quarter-kilo of mostly sweet black cherries and one perfectly round musk melon that I could tell was ripe to the core from the effusive scent that hung over the fruit cart, tampering with the scents of the other fruits.

Your kitchen is dysfunctional. The stove is moody, the microwave sings, the toaster regularly goes on strike, and the sink is so low I have to bend to wash the rice which I then soak. Your water heater is the only reliable appliance. I heat two cups of water, for the pulao. I dice an onion, a large, majestic one. It yields to my touch, and for the first time in a long while, my eyes aren't overwhelmed by its pungent perfumes. I grate a tomato so that the fleshy red fruit is now a wet, thin pulp.

Heat a casserole pot. Preferably non-stick so the rice doesn't cling to the bottom. Add a tablespoon of oil. Allow it to warm through. Remember this as if it were formula: 5 pieces of clove, 7 peppercorns, 4 pieces of cardamom, an inch-long thick stick of cinnamon, a bay leaf. Let them sizzle in the oil. Add the diced onion and let it fry well to the point of disintegration. Let the grated tomato splash in the oil. Stir. Wait and watch the separation. Add stock. Deconstruct it. Stir. Add rice, stir-fry. Add the two cups of hot water. Add salt according to instinct. Cover the casserole with a lid, leaving a tiny gap for the steam to escape. Cook until each grain of rice grows in size and softens.

For you, only excess. Because when you bite into food that is good, your body crumbles. And with every morsel, I dismantle you until you submit to my sliver-of-a-touch.

Because any man who kisses the way you do, with controlled abandon, as if transporting a ball of fire from your lips onto mine...is deserving of a feast...

Take my firm black-cherry-coloured body. Undress the layers of cloth that surround me like a peel. There are various methods of preparation to choose from. You could have me simmer in the brazen warmth of your touch; or use red-wine as marinade, leave me intoxicated for hours until I ooze. But tonight, I suggest you eat me raw. Place my unfurled body on an un-made bed, bite into the dark, supple flesh. Start with the nape of my neck until you reach the tips of my toes. Play with your food; let your fingers graze against my nipples, the curve of my belly, the incline of my ass. Suck on the joints, chew on my skin. Consume me.

For you, a feast.

Indian, international, Goan!

Wendell Rodricks

Wendell Rodricks is a fashion designer by profession and environmental activist by accident. He lives in Colvale village and writes occasionally on fashion, history and all things Goan.

'Put your country and your roots in your

clothes,' she said, as I walked out, portfolio in hand. This was a very chic Madame at Yves Saint Laurent showing me the door.

I sat on the tunnel ridge where Princess Diana would tragically die a few years later. I felt deflated. An empty, crumpled brown paper shopping bag. Ignoring the drizzle, I crossed the *Pont de l'Alma* Bridge. The *Tour Eiffel* was out of focus. With my tears.

That night after a hot *soupe de poisson* and a fresh *baguette*, I stared at the pale blue ceiling of my room, oblivious to the television and the chirpy French voice on *La Roue de la Fortune*. I detested this game in Los Angeles. But here in Paris, it was not Vana White with her chicklet teeth who spun the white spaces, revealing letters to form a phrase, a name, a place, an object. It was Annie Pujol. Wheel of Fortune *a la française* taught me French.

What had she said at YSL?

'Your sketches are very good, Monsieur *Rodreeks*. But why don't I see your beautiful Indian *hereetaage* in your work? Why will Monsieur Saint Laurent need an intern to design dresses and skirts and jackets? He does that very well himself, *n'est ce pas?*'

Point taken. Defeat accepted.

It was time to leave this beautiful city. Say '*au revoir*' humbly. Go back to India, go home. Look at my work from the outside. Soul search on the inside. Create clothes that looked Indian, Goan, nationally new, internationally acceptable.

A very determined man boarded an Air France flight a fortnight later. The day was 15th August 1988. Auspicious! Time to let freedom ring in a new fashion language on my sketch pad.

Dr. Kalindi Randeri, Principal at the Premlila Vithaldas Polytechnic, Shrimati Nathibhai Damodardas Thackersay Women's University, had written to me while I was in Paris. 'We are the only fashion college in India. Would you consider teaching? The salary is nothing. But you will meet many people and …India needs people like you.'

I limped into the Mumbai fashion scene. Taught three days a week at SNDT Women's University. World Costume History. Pattern Making. Fashion Co-ordination. The lecture platform terrorized me. There were thirty pairs of eyes trained on every move I made, like well honed missiles. Waiting for a slip-up. To giggle. To mock. To challenge. Fear clutched at my throat.

All anxiety evaporated in a mere minute – from the moment I looked at my first slide. I loved that platform. It gave me a sense of power. At the end of the lecture, my ears imagined applause. This was an ego trip!

During recess, I would learn the Indian History of Costume. Tea breaks became library breaks. I read Pupul Jayakar's 'The Earthen Drum' ten times over to study tribal and folk art. Borrowed students' journals to differentiate *Kantha* embroidery stitches from *Phulkari*. A giddy gaggle of girls would drape a Bengali dhoti over my jeans. On off days I visited the cloth bazaars and the sole designer boutique in Mumbai, Ensemble. Timidly pushed open the plush doors. Pawed through racks of rich clothes. Bright silks with embroidery. 'Can I help you Sir?' 'No, thank you, just browsing.' For clues on what I should never design. I could not identify with the bright colours, the excess and the volume.

When a new boutique opened in the swish Kemp's Corner, they called. 'Hello, this is Nancy Chopra. We are opening a new designer boutique, Glitterati. Would you like to display your label?' I did not have a label, and was in no rush to start one. Madame Yves Saint Laurent's words rang in my years. 'Do not do what exists. Create your own philosophy which speaks of your roots and looks fresh in India and internationally.' *Oui, Madame.* The label can wait.

So I freelanced and began to work part time at Garden Vareli. At the Garden studio, I began to think of a line of clothes. With the support of Shilpa Shah who owned Garden Silk Mills, Dr Kalindi Randeri, choreographer Jeannie Naoroji's encouragement and a big push from designer Hemant Trevedi (who also taught at SNDT), I did a line of twelve garments. Actually, there were twelve tunics and just six pairs of palazzo pants. Budget restraints. The models at the end of the lineup had to wait 'bottomless' in the wings and rip off the palazzos from the girls exiting. Journalist Meher Castelino fawned over the collection in an entire page in Mid-Day. My parents who were puzzled at my career choices reacted with suitable awe. 'You have a full page in the papers.' Excuse me? 'Yes a full page...with photographs and sketches. And it is a rave review!' Fame arrived at my threshold that day.

In two years, it did not matter whether the clothes were made in Bombay or Timbuktu. Fashionistas crowed about the humble cottons, the minimal approach, the lack of embellishment and the finish so fine that the clothes could be worn inside out. In the sea of colour and embroidery on racks nationwide, these were the only clothes that were 'different'. Which meant that not many people were going to dare to be different. The trickle turned into a stream. And finally into a river. Following my heart, quite unconsciously, I gave India Minimalism.

In 1993, I moved to Goa. 'Mad!' they said. 'Professional suicide!' 'Just when his stars are looking up...'

In Colvale village, soul searching was the easiest exercise. Villagers were baffled as to why a city boy came to a village to work. Emilia Zuzarte, posed her cherubic self on our common wall - 'So you are going to make clothes in this rain?' Indeed I was…with one tailor.

A week later we recruited two village girls. It upset them to no end when after a hard day's work they would be told 'Open it and do it again. The seams are bad.' They cried each time we uttered the word 'Reopen'. Within three years however they knew they were the best seamstresses in the country. They would beam proudly when buyers from Paris or New York would exclaim 'these village girls did this finishing? Incredible!'

Being close to nature, the first collection I did in Goa was called 'Prodigale' (The Prodigal Colvalkar had returned home). We wove silk with banana fiber, cotton with pineapple fiber, coarse unbleached cotton in colours such as dull olive, dusty brown and pale grey. And we accessorized the collection with coconut-shell ear-rings and bracelets crafted with love by Franco in Camurlim. They went from sleepy Colvale to enjoy the spotlight in urban Bombay. It was unheard of at that time… that a designer could work in a remote village and show in the main fashion metros. The Prodigale Collection hit all the right notes. Words like ecofriendly, asymmetric and rural couture were liberally used in reviews. The asymmetric cuts came from the way the sari draped across the bodice. The men's kurta shirt was born out of practicality and the ambition to strip down the Indian kurta, such that it was bare of collar, cuff and placket. The sensual drape was inspired by the backless cholis on Lambadi women who collected used bottles in Colvale.

Well, Madame YSL, India was now in the clothes.

There was Goa waiting to be addressed. Waiting in the wings for her turn in the warmth of the arc lights. How do we put the wind, the breeze, the sea, the calm, the spiritual peace into the clothes?

Over time, the Goan influences appeared in various avatars. In my mind, I was very clear that when someone wore the garments, they should go on a virtual Goan holiday. The chiffons should feel like sea spray. The cotton should feel as light as summer breeze on a river. Silk should glide on sun kissed skin. *Sossegado* should drape the wearer. Sunlight should illuminate the body in pure white.

Twenty two years later, I look back at that day when rain and tears poured on the *Pont de l'Alma*. Thanks to Yves Saint Laurent, the tears have turned to those of pride and joy. To stand alongside the best in the world and truthfully say that the clothes are created with a creative heart in a blessed land. That they found an international wearability despite their humble Goan origins. They traveled the world and enjoyed the best ramps on the planet. In Peking, Shanghai, Düsseldorf, Dubai, Paris, New York. We showed twice in Paris. On invitation. Once to the world's best fair. The *Salon du Prêt-à-Porter de Paris*.

I went to invite the lady at Yves Saint Laurent. Sadly she had left, since the famous label was sold to Gucci. I wanted to thank her for sending me back to India. And to tell her that I do make the clothes from my heart, keeping India and Goa as inspiration. And that the clothes are made humbly but proudly in a Goan village called Colvale.

The unsolved mystery of a family portrait

Fatima da Silva Gracias

Fatima da Silva Gracias has written on health, hygiene and food from a historical perspective in Goa, and in this process has also kaleidoscoped the role of women in this land that she loves much.

A few years ago, a cousin from the USA was

down in Goa on a visit. She showed me a copy of an old family photograph and said: 'Keep it, your dad and grandparents are there.' At that
time, she was taking back photographs for her American nieces, who
wished to know all about their Goan roots.

I recalled seeing the original black and white photograph hanging
on the wall of a *sala* in my paternal grandmother's family home. I had
recognised the grand uncles (brothers of my grandmother) but I had not

paid much attention to the children squatting on the floor, until another cousin pointed out 'One of the kids is your dad'. It is the only photograph I have of my grandparents, father and his siblings together.

Then one day, as I was sitting in my study reminiscing on the past, I remembered the photo. I took it out from my collection and studied it at leisure. Several questions came to my mind:

Who were the adults in the photograph?
Who were the children in the photo besides my father?
When was the photo taken?
What was the occasion?

The backdrop of this photograph is the compound wall of my grandmother's family home in the 'village of the lakes'. In the photo, six of the men are in formal western style suits, the patriarch – my great grandfather (seated in the middle) is wearing a bow tie. His eldest son – a priest (sitting third from right) and one of the twin sons – a seminarian (standing first left) are in cassocks. Some of them have hats with them, placed on their laps (not on their heads!). A style of the times? Two of the young grand uncles sport walking sticks as well. Was this a symbol of authority or again in the manner of that period?

Avó - my grandmother (sitting second left) is in a native costume – an embroidered *Fota Quimão* or *Torhop-baz* which she wore on formal occasions until the 1940's. Later she changed to western style dress when she began to have difficulty in walking in a *Pano baju* due to a leg fracture caused by a fall. As a child, I remember seeing in her *armario* (wardrobe) a beautiful *Fota* made of red velvet with embroidered border in gold thread, kept wrapped in a soft white cloth. In this picture, Avó's aunt (seated third left) is also wearing a similar *Fota*. This outfit was worn by some Goan women, particularly of Salcete, from the second half of the nineteenth century until the middle of the twentieth. My Avó's sister (sitting first left) is in western style full length dress with a long necklace hanging down her front.

Could this photograph have been taken at a family reunion? Perhaps when the second daughter, (the one in western style dress) was going to marry the man she fell in love with and not the man chosen by her family?

In those days, marriages were arranged by parents, relatives or a *raibari* – a matchmaker. Young people rarely fell in love and married the person of their choice. Normally marriages took place within one's caste and community. Girls were given a dowry, and those of privileged families were bestowed both in cash and in kind. Under the prevalent Portuguese law, women had equal right to their family property. But very often parents avoided leaving their married daughters their rightful share of ancestral wealth on the grounds that they were given a dowry, which was much less than what they were entitled to. At the time of marriage, it was a practice among landed families to ask the daughter to sign a *desistencia*, a paper giving up her right to the share of her parent's property. In many families, some sons and daughters were left unmarried at home, to prevent the division of properties.

My grand aunt must have been strong-willed to go against the wishes of the patriarch and her formidable older siblings to marry the man of her choice. Her daughter, who is a nun and now well in her mid eighties tells me that her mother married a tall handsome Goan working in Africa, soon after World War I. Goans had begun migrating to Africa in significant numbers from the nineteenth century due to lack of job opportunities and a moribund economy.

The man my grand aunt married was no stranger to her. He was the widower of her younger sister, who had died in Africa after giving birth to a girl – the child seated on the floor third from left in this picture. The family was not keen on sending another daughter to Africa. Yellow fever was endemic in the region where the tall man worked. It is also possible that the family wished to maintain the tradition of keeping a daughter unmarried at home. Who knows! Eventually the newly married bride did not migrate to Africa, instead her husband returned to Goa for good after some time.

I carried the photograph with me when I visited my ancestral home and showed it to Tio Julio, my father's youngest sibling and the youngest child in this photo. I was excited. I had so many questions to ask him:

Who were the adults in the photograph?

Who were the children in the photo besides my father?

When was the photo taken?

What was the occasion?

I have memories of five out of six *Tios Avos* (grand uncles). 'This is *Tio Aleixo...Tio-Padre...the priest*' said Tio Julio pointing to the man seated third from right. He was the grand uncle I never knew, who died much before I was born. I had heard stories about him from the family. He came across as a strict disciplinarian, who was fastidious about cleanliness. His young nephews and even the adults in the family would be pulled up if a bit of paper or chocolate wrapping was found on the floor. Everyone was scared of him.

Some of my grand uncles joined the nearby Rachol Seminary for their studies. One went to study medicine in Bombay and gave up the course half way. In most Goan Christian families of that time, traditionally the first son became a priest, the second one married and the remaining sons stayed unmarried at home. In this family of nine children, the first son became a priest, the second son remained a bachelor and the third son married (sitting extreme right) during their father's life time. Eventually, the other three sons also married.

We children did not have much contact with the powerful (within the family!) second brother (sitting second from right) of my Avó. He was considered proud and '*esturrado*' by some. He visited us twice or thrice a year in his small car and brought us mangoes and other fruits during the season. I remember one Christmas season when this grand uncle visited our home in Canacona where my father was involved in an anti-malaria campaign. He brought us some toys including a toy gramophone with batteries – a novelty for us, a colourful miniature of the one we had at home. We were thrilled!'

Squatting on the ground in the middle is your Tio C,' said Tio Julio. *'Your Pai is next to him. Second from left is Tio A, you know even as a small boy he liked to dress well, he was always conscious of his appearance and spent a lot of time in front of the mirror,'* reminisced Tio Julio. *'This is Tio Claudio to the extreme right, who studied with me at the seminary. He would often fall sick and died young during the Second World War. His death was a hard blow to Papa and Mama.'*

Is this your grandmother? I asked.

'No, no, she is not,' replied Tio Julio, *'None of us ever met our grandmother. She died at the dawn of the twentieth century, just days after giving birth to twin boys. That's them, standing at both corners in the photograph.'*

In those days maternity deaths were high in Goa due to lack of medical facilities and transport.

Tio Julio continued, *'This lady you are pointing out is Moga Tia (Erminia), one of the two unmarried sisters of my grandfather. She was the one who looked after my mother and her siblings after the death of their mother. Moga Tia was good at cooking and it was from her that her nieces and some nephews learnt cooking and to appreciate good food.*

'And here's my Papa – your Avô, standing second from left. Can you see that portrait on the wall? This group photograph and that portrait were probably made at the same time.'

Avô, my grandfather, had changed a good deal from the time this photo was taken to the times I remember him. He had not only aged but also shrunk in height. I have vivid memories of my paternal grandparents – the only grandparents my sister, brother and I knew. The Avô that I remember was of medium height, pale, soft spoken and a man of few words. He too had a twin brother. I wonder if they looked alike. We have no photo of Avô's twin. Both qualified to be teachers, towards the end of

the nineteenth century, and we still have their diplomas. People of my
father's generation in our village remembered Avô as a very good teacher.
My Avô's twin had his first teaching assignment at Sanguem and died
there of snake bite which was a common occurrence in those areas. In
those days it was a practice to send newly appointed government em-
ployees to far off places like Daman, Diu, Dadra, Nagara Haveli or some
remote areas of the 'Novas Conquistas' territories in Goa.

We were told that Avô had his first heart attack in his sixties. After
that he did not move much outdoors. He loved to sing, and loved cheese.
Occasionally, he would tell us stories in Konkani and Portuguese. We
noticed that in the last years of his life, if he did not wish to answer a
question, he would reply that he did not remember. We knew this was
just an excuse. He could be adamant too, for instance if we requested
him to repeat a song he had just finished singing. If not in a mood, he
would not sing, however much we pleaded. His trademark was a bonnet
and a walking stick. He owned three sticks, including an unusual one my
father brought him from Diu. The stick was covered with strands of tiny
multicoloured beads.

At home, Avô spent time on a *cadeira á Voltaire* (rocking chair).
People were always dropping in, to seek advice on property and
Comunidade matters, from my Avô and his youngest son Julio. Then
one day, towards the end of April when he was ninety years old, Avô
collapsed while washing his hands and slowly fell to the ground. His was
the first funeral I attended.

My conversation with Tio Julio came to an abrupt end when he
told me '*Don't expect me to remember all the details at my age, I don't remember the occasion. The photo was taken so long ago, I was a little child. And you
see, soon I will be 90 years old.*'

Now I knew who the adults and children were, but I still needed
answers to the remaining questions:

When was the photo taken?

What was the occasion?

I wish I had paid more attention when my father talked about this branch of the family. I asked my father's cousin who lives in the family house now (his father is seated extreme right) if he had any information regarding the picture. He does not; neither do other cousins of his generation, who had recently gathered for his eightieth birthday celebration.

Could the family have gathered specially for a photo sitting? I asked and they all said it could be a possibility. In those days, they did sit for a photo shoot of the family when the family met on some festive occasion or when married daughters came home with their family to spend holidays.

In the early years of her married life my Avó – the eldest daughter of her family, her husband – my Avô and their five sons would spend part of their summer holidays at her father's home. They would travel in a *machila*, a wooden palanquin that took more than four hours to reach the destination including the resting time given to the *boyas*, the machila bearers. Our father often related an incident during one such holiday. A messenger had arrived from their village with a letter from the parish priest asking my grandfather to return to the village. A directive had been received from Church authorities, that the miraculous image of Our Lady of Livramento worshipped by many should be placed in the chapel of the ward. The image was in a house chapel nearby and the owner of the house had recently died without leaving any children. The house was closed. My Avô being her closest relative was asked to come back to do the needful. Avô, my father and his eldest sibling returned home much before their holidays were over.

Avó married in her late teens. A bit late, according to the tradition of the time when girls were married in their early teens, despite the law that banned child marriages. Later in life her disability prevented Avó from moving out much, yet she managed the affairs of the house well until her eighties. She was strong and had her way on many occasions. In this connection, an image that comes to my mind was of my Avó dressed in a sky blue georgette sari, all ready to go out. Her sons were surprised to see her all dressed up for a festive occasion; after all she had lost her brother a little over two months back and according to tradition she was supposed to wear mourning garb, a black outfit. But Avó was clear in her mind and she told her sons firmly '*It is true I lost my brother, but Guilherme is like a son to me, neighbours are as good as family. How can I stay away on this occasion which means so much to them, they are always there for us. I would like to wish the couple and give my blessings.*' And so she did go with us to the wedding but returned soon after fulfilling her obligations.

Women of my grandmother's generation lived with grace and were not as disempowered as it is made to seem. I remember Avó loved to keep in touch with various relatives and friends. Since there were no telephones and she could not move easily unless my father offered a lift, she often kept in touch with her people through a messenger or her youngest son.

Early in the Twenties and the period of the Great Depression were difficult and expensive times for my grandparents. They had to raise five sons and provide them with education. My grandfather's earnings were small and the coconuts from their palm groves did not fetch much in the market then. They were helped in the education of their children by my Avó's younger brothers.

In Goa, in the past, sons usually followed in the profession of their elders. My eldest uncle decided to be a teacher like his father and joined the *Escola Normal* and studied English as well. English education helped him to get a job at Mogadishu in Somalia. From there, he moved to Uganda where he worked for a British bank. He was wise enough to send two of his children to a boarding school in England, sell his house and seek his transfer to London before the take over of Uganda by Idi Amin.

During one of his last visits to Goa from London, this affable uncle of ours told me this interesting story. In Somalia, away from his close knit family, he felt lonely and expressed a desire to marry. This was soon after World War II. The family in Goa arranged his marriage with a doctor's daughter who had studied English. Photos were exchanged and sent to Africa. But my uncle could not come to Goa, to see and marry the girl selected for him because of the political situation back in Africa. The parents of the girl were not prepared to send their young unmarried girl to Africa without a marriage ceremony.

How to have a wedding ceremony without a groom? Church and civil officials were contacted. The family was advised to let the prospective groom grant a Power of Attorney to a member of the family in Goa. My uncle sent the document to my Avó's second unmarried brother to represent him at the church and at the civil ceremonies. On the wedding day, a lunch was hosted for close relatives. During this lunch the uncle who represented the groom asked mischievously, to one and all whether he was not entitled to the rights of a married man!

Pai - my father and second son of the family, followed the profession of his paternal great grandfather. While his ancestor was given *Carta pela sua Magestade* to practice medicine, my father graduated from Goa Medical School and went for further studies to Portugal. He did well and was awarded a gold medal and later a scholarship by W.H.O. for studies in malaria. Unlike many boys of his times he came back to Goa, joined the medical cadre and married his childhood sweetheart, the youngest of four daughters of a government official. My father loved books, spent his free time reading, listening to the radio and in later years watching television He and my mother encouraged us to read, even though the choice of books were limited.

Let's come back to the remaining three younger grand uncles that feature in this photograph. The eldest of the three, let's call him Tio N, the one who had studied in Bombay, (standing second from the right) and the twins – Tios C and D, moved out of their family home after the death of their father in the 1920's. Although they had strong bonds with their home, they also had dreams of their own, perhaps of starting their own families. Apparently, they were also weary of too much authority. This move was the beginning of a rift that took years to mend. They settled in Bardez, across the Mandovi River. Tios N and C set up a successful business. Among all these three grand uncles, I was more familiar with Tio D. Every year he would spend a fortnight at our home. I recall he would arrive in his brownish linen suit and a hat. We children were amused to see him spending a great deal of time in front of the mirror, arranging and rearranging the few strands of hair left on his crown.

Tio N, who married my mother's beautiful second sister, moved to Panjim and lived by a road that had only six houses at that time. Two of their neighbours were German spies who were made famous by the movie 'Sea Wolves'. By the 1950's, winds of change were blowing in Goa. There was an upsurge in the Goan freedom struggle as a result of British India gaining independence. Goans from Goa and Africa were moving in new directions in search of better pastures. Tio N's two boys migrated to Brazil – one of whom recently published a book: As Aventuras, Viagens e Historias de um Imigrante. Two daughters migrated to the US. The eldest son was involved in Goa's freedom struggle. The family in Goa was under pressure then. Tio N and Tia E decided to move to Brazil, a little before Goa became a part of the Indian Union.

When was the photo taken?

What was the occasion?

Who will tell? Will I ever get an answer? None of the living cousins of my father's generation have a clue. All of them are the children of my grand uncles and aunt in the photo but they were born much after the photo was taken. At the recent family gathering some of us had another look at the original photo. It has been moved to the entrance of the house. No person in the photograph is alive today. The youngest, my Tio Julio died two years ago. The little girl Ernestina in the photo also died around the same time.

It is my guess that this group photograph was taken between 1918 and 1920. Maybe just before the second daughter married the tall Goan working in Africa. I have come to this conclusion based on the age of the youngest child in the photo – Tio Julio, who was born in July 1917; he must have been a year and half old or at the most two years old when the photo was taken. But what was the occasion? That remains to this day an unresolved mystery!

Into the dark heart

Prava Rai

Prava Rai lives on a mysterious island that drifts in and out of the fog on the Mandovi River. She is familiar with the parmal of Goa, and continues to seek Goa's elusive fragrance, clearing the overgrowth of modernity to seek the flowers that bloom unseen.

It has been a little over a year since I left

Chorão, my home in Goa and relocated myself in Kodaikanal. Bouts of homesickness overwhelm me sometimes and I long to get back to the warm embrace of Goa. On chilly mornings when the ground outside glitters with frost, I find my longing unbearable.

My thoughts take me back to my island home. Very often chance acquaintances exclaim, 'How lovely! You live on an island? Tell us what it is like to live there?'

What shall I dwell on? What shall I recall? The beauty of the island? The peace and quiet? The ancient chapels and churches and remnants of a glorious past? The crumbling edifices, reminders of past pride and present humiliation? Or past humiliation and present confidence? And the legends and rumours that abound in every hillock and valley and lane of this beautiful island?

My mind takes me to mapless territories.

Early morning walks on the island have led me to streets lined by stately but empty homes and open fields and calm creeks. I have heard *bhajans* emanating from sheds attached to these desolate homes. I hear the sinuous strains pervading the rooms, empty except for framed photographs commemorating milestones like marriages and graduation and the tilted altar overhung with cobwebs and stained by mildew. I have met nostalgic expatriates arriving occasionally to peer in through barred windows perhaps trying to decipher and reclaim the memories of homes abandoned long ago for alien lands.

During a recent visit home from Kodaikanal I was ushered into the dark heart of Chorão once more – glimpses of which I have seen in the past. I have always shied away from exploring these disturbing clues that have lain in the quiet corners of my mind. Within this idyllic paradise there is a heart that beats to dark and fearful dreams. Certainly no one from the outside, neither tourists nor those who dwell on mainland Goa, will have access into this terrain.

'I have to go for a funeral,' said our driver, Anand, who has been with us for the many years we've lived in Chorão.

Whose funeral? Who died?

Jane.

Who is she?

One of my classmates, from St. Bartholomew High School.

Then she cannot be very old? What happened?

They found her body floating in the family well this morning.

She had committed suicide. She lived with her widowed mother. Anand is not normally garrulous and to get information out of him is like prising open a reluctant clam. But today, something moved him.

'Jane was a good girl and a good student,' he said. 'But she had been suffering. Over the years, she had withdrawn into herself, slowly cut herself off, even the neighbours hardly saw her. Occasionally she would go to the chapel on Sundays – for the early morning mass where there were fewer worshippers. She seemed to shun company,' he explained.

As it often happens in small communities there is acceptance of changes in familiar neighbours and the community adjusts and leaves the odd one alone. Not ever interfering, just accepting her turn of character.

We were on the ferry the next day. Anand gets a call on his mobile.

I hear his surprised and shocked response and when he finally puts away his phone he turns to me.

Today Kavita will not come to work.

Why?

Last night her husband, Shekhar, committed suicide.

A suicide again? Within a span of a couple of days, two suicides on this island paradise!

Later I visit Kavita at her small house beside the paddy field. The *tulsi vrindavan* outside the house is surrounded by overturned *kollashe*, earthen pots. There are two men sitting on plastic chairs in the narrow verandah. They are solemn and tearless.

A woman, a neighbour, takes me in. I find Kavita on the bed leaning against the wall. Her face drawn and her eyes dry with pain. She is a statuesque woman. Always dressed impeccably in cheerful saris and a big red bindi on the forehead, her hair neatly coiffed into a bun at the nape of her neck and a string of jasmine or rose or hibiscus tucked neatly into it.

But this is not the Kavita I knew.

I sit beside her on the bed; the only chair is occupied by Maria, a friend, who has arrived to offer condolence.

I ask Kavita, 'What happened?' 'I don't know,' she moans. There is a young woman sitting beside her, also exhausted and shocked. She is Kavita's daughter.

She tells me that her father had swallowed poison while the family slept in the house. They found his body outside the house in the morning. He had taken this extreme step because he could not repay an old debt, she said. He had originally taken a bank loan to buy a vehicle for hire. He made good money but was still unable to repay the loan. Years ago, with the bank demanding repayment and having defaulted several times, he went to Santan, an old friend, for help. Santan helped him clear the loan at the bank on the understanding that

Shekhar would now repay him the amount.

But years rolled by and the repayment was only made in infre-quent dribs and drabs. Finally Shekhar managed to repay the princi-pal but the interest remained due.

There were frequent recriminations. Kavita worked hard. The vehicle meanwhile was disposed of, and Shekhar found himself a job. But the matter of the loan still remained. The last reminder from Santan sent Kavita in a flurry begging him to give her time and that she would repay the debt somehow. Santan, exasperated and tired of long years of waiting for his hard-earned money, told her that he did not know her and his business was with Shekhar.

She left with tear-filled eyes and a heart heaving with apprehen-sion.

So finally this was the end of the matter. At fifty, Kavita's husband committed suicide, probably unable to bear the humiliation and face the impossibility of ever being able to repay the debt.

The other day, I am told once again that they had been searching for a missing man. He had gone fishing and did not return. Alerted by his brother, neighbours arrived with torches and combed the island but did not find him. Early next morning his body washed up at the Sodotim sluice gate. They assumed it was another case of suicide.

Unfathomable loneliness, unpaid debts and yet other reasons drive dozens of people each year to take their own lives on this island. For a small community living in idyllic surroundings, these suicides are omi-nous warnings of a people in pain.

Unaware of these undercurrents in the troubled community and enchanted by the island we bought a piece of land and built a house, to put down roots, perhaps. When we moved to our new house it was surrounded by tangled undergrowth of weeds and thorny vines as well as tall mango and teak trees and dozens of kajra and a few exquisite kokum trees. I tried naively to clear the land of tangled roots. After struggling for three days, despite being helped by Sonu and Shantaram, I gave up. The roots had entangled so impossibly, the thorny ones with others, that we were unable to distinguish the good from the bad. With angry scratches all over my hands and with aching muscles, I gave up. I let the roots be.

Undeterred and forgetful of the initial attempts I have since been struggling with the land, trying to disentangle old roots and nurture new ones.

Recently a friend managed to coax Vasu, Rajen, Mohan and Ramakant to work on our land. I feel becalmed and joyous now watching these men work, work in harmony with each other. I can sense their affinity with the plants and saplings that have taken root almost inadvertently. People familiar with new horticultural practices discourage saplings that grow from the natural falling of seeds on the ground and advise grafts. I am not very good at pulling out these accidental, yet natural 'life surges'. When I saw Vasu lovingly dig around some of these saplings today, and say gently, '*Ye bore asai, hanh?*' as he gently patted the soil around the roots, I had no heart to tell him otherwise.

I wandered off, feeling a sense of peace.

(Some names have been changed)

Petticoat pride

Savia Viegas

*Savia Viegas has recently retired from dog-walking under doctor's advice
and now only writes, paints and runs a pre-primary school in Carmona.*

Aninha Maria Antonette Falcão of Cuncolim

came across the river as Belarmino's bride, she was twelve and he thirty.
She came from an old family whose men had traditionally worked in
white-collar jobs in Africa. Their house located in Mileamvaddo was
identified by a staircase of twenty five steps that led up to the entrance.
Sitting on the steps the quarter residents would beat drums for the Sal to
subside when the river rose at the height of monsoon and villagers would
tremble, fearing it would submerge the village.

They were eight siblings and she, the second youngest, bore the
insecurity of having been brought up in the shadow of an absentee father. 'Better a bride from one of our own Saxtti villages,' reasoned Argentina after she had scrutinised the proposal and clinched the marriage. 'All the better if she is from Cuncolim or Velim. Who knows what
can happen! Belarmino lives in Panjim and the Panjim girls are all
pamprelles. They have feet to dance and hands and eyes to flirt, not to
work like us Saxtti women. We Saxtti women scrape the earth with our
hands and turn mud into gold. '

So the choice was Aninha Antonette. They brought her trousseau
in a Macao chest across the Sal, then black *boyas* carried it across the
paind, a shallow depressed walkway, to Carmona. These painds were cool
to walk in and made the weight of the palanquin easier to carry. Cut in
such a way so as to trap the wind, they offered some relief from the hot

sun so that walking three or four kilometres was made more bearable.

Later the boyas carried Aninha in a wedding palanquin on the same path, panting in unison, their dark bare bodies glistening with beads of sweat.

'Oi, oi, oi,' they chanted as they trotted.

The chant of the boyas as they carried the palanquin, the heat of the summer sun, the sandy painds, the stiff tulle of her dress, the alien feel and smell of powder on her face and above all the naiveté of her childhood and the sequence of events unfolding brought her much confusion. The matchmaker, the proposal, her mother, her uncles, her mother portioning out her linen and sovereigns, all flashed in her mind. She touched the gold sovereigns with king heads in the clasp around her neck. Her father had bought them a long time ago when her youngest brother was born, before he disappeared, as whisper held it, with an African woman. Others said he was bewitched by the charms of a Zambesi heiress he worked for and after she had dispensed with her white husband, she kept him tied to her bedpost.

'African women have huge breasts,' her mother would say, gesticulating absurdly by holding her bodice. 'They use them to trap Goan men.'

'Assim,' she would indicate holding the bodice again.

Aninha was a mere child when she was married. The only thing she did very well was swim like a fish. She was, as they say, são muito simples e são idiota. The wedding ceremony was simple, for Argentina considered such expenditure a waste. She explained to all that she was a widow and it would be inauspicious for her to launch grand festivities when the bones of her husband were still disintegrating in his grave. A few of the bride's family and some zonnkar families from Velim were the wedding guests. Those who were invited remembered the wedding long afterward. The meal followed a traditional course; crab soup, meat stew, pulao aromated with the spices that had been included in Aninha Antonette's dowry and caramel pudding and china grass custard decorated with sunflowers, served in small helpings.

The house, incomplete at that time, was almost threadbare, for it was a practice among thrifty Goan families to expand their houses with the turn of family fortunes. The kitchen and the store rooms to store rice silos would be built first; then would come the bedrooms, with maybe a *saleta* for small functions. But all the while its structure would be built strong. Last to be built would be the huge hall with a balcao and a wood-work veranda with exterior embellishments which would be visible markers of the family's status within the village and community.

Somewhere in the middle of the festivities Aninha had lost track of the celebrations going on around her. The guests had settled into their own grooves while she had not yet familiarised herself with the new surroundings. She began taking off her clothes; the heavy satin gown with a crochet bodice, the bone-lace yardages of her petticoats which added awkwardness to her walk. She remembered Tia Anita making them all through the night in what seemed a strange act of sorcery. She stuck pins, rolled the pillow around, adjusted the threads, changed the cards and soon yards of lace were billowing forth from such movements.

Aninha's face stood out sharply, small and pointed in what seemed to be like a vase-on-doily-still-life. Around her diminutive form was a confusion of lace, pineapple motifs and hearts, all trapped and crystallised in a filet net. Not being able to keep pace with all that was happening around her, she took off the rest of the offending garments and started playing with the younger friends who had come as part of the bridal entourage. They fetched a bit of charcoal and broken bits of tile from somewhere, and drawing squares on the floor, began to play 'saat fatranim'.

Argentina never forgave her daughter-in-law this slur and to an extent that sealed the pact between the son and the mother over the building of family fortunes in which Aninha was always to remain an outsider. She gave birth to eight children of whom only four babies survived full term. Some were born in the seventh month. Several attempts would be made to help them survive. The umbilical cord would not be cut and the placenta would be placed in hot water to give the baby heat. If labour began in the eighth month then the mourning would start before the birth, for all knew that an eighth month baby never survived. Francis died when he was a year old. Belarmino said he developed bronchitis because he had been kept in the open air immediately and too long after a bath and the finger of accusation pointed to Aninha who had done it. After Francis's death she suffered from depression for several months.

She had lost four of her babies. The burden of eight pregnancies had taken its toll. For eight months she slept in the old room, the *porne quarto* where Argentina had trapped the tiger. His paw scratch marks and his nasal excrement were permanently impressed on the wooden safety door. Aninha tossed and turned all day long, ate her meals and went back to sleep. It was this lethal hibernation that now gave her body its distinctive outline: a frail diminutive body with a huge distended stomach that looked like paddy piled after harvest.

A strong wall of silence had settled between Belarmino and Aninha. They hardly spoke to each other. The last exchange of words took place when he came home one afternoon and Aninha prepared a bowl of ragi porridge and left it for him on the dining table. The bowl was uncovered and a fly navigating over the contents of the ragi porridge slipped and fell into the bowl. Belarmino was a stickler for clean habits and could not tolerate Aninha's sloppiness.

'Aninha,' he screamed.

'What happened,' she came and asked nonchalantly.

'How many times have I told you not to leave food uncovered…a fly has fallen in.'

'So what,' she said, fishing it out with her finger and depositing the carcass in the basin.

'Have it now, it's out!' Aninha told her husband matter-of-factly.

He then took the bowl of warm ragi porridge and banged it on her head. The bowl cracked. The still-warm sticky mass leaked down her hair along with the oozing blood onto her face. That evening after the doctor had stitched the wound, Aninha packed her clothes and went through the fields to the river bank. She hailed the boatman, paid him, and he ferried her to the other side to her maternal home in Cuncolim. Several months passed. Belarmino didn't stir to visit her and she didn't come back. Argentina looked after the children and Belarmino got en-grossed in grafting his mango trees. His splicing method showed such great success that he tried the same process on other fruit-bearing trees: chikoo, guava and custard apple. The fruits got sweeter and more lus-cious. Eight months passed. Aninha did not return.

She was now at her mother's home and the urge to get back into the water often possessed her with manic urgency. But a strange lethargy had overtaken her since her return to Cuncolim and she quietly read-justed to playing the assistant to her younger sister-in–law. She sewed, chopped vegetables, crocheted and cleaned the house. But fate offered her a strange opportunity not only to indulge in her childhood pastime, but also to return back to her marital home.

Her return to Carmona was dramatic. She swam back in her petti-coat. Aninha had been a swimmer since her childhood. An arm of the Sal River ran by her house and the *vodd* running from Fatorpa to the Sal River and the Arabian Sea was also very close. Swimming was the only activity that offered her security in childhood and made her forget her fears. She would swim for hours and hours, never tiring of the water. Despite her mother's admonitions, she even bathed in the river. That bond with water had ceased with her marriage and with a child born every year till she was twenty, there were very few occasions to visit her maternal home and revel in its childhood pleasures.

This was the time that the Ranes had intensified their attacks on the wealthy southern villages of Velim, Cuncolim and Chinchinim. The

Ranes were the rulers of Satari, a border state of Goa whose territory had been captured by the Portuguese. Revolting against this annexation, the Ranes indulged in banditry and made incursions into the wealthy settlements of the colonised territory. These prosperous villages were targeted very often. Looting and pillaging, the bandits terrorised the settled populations. The most tangible wealth which they could lay hands on of course was gold. The wealthy villagers kept their gold in the oddest of places: at the bottom of silos, in the well, in a hole in the ground or even underneath the hearth in a specially built chamber.

Cornelia, a rich woman from one of the southern villages, however was caught unawares. The Rane bandits entered her house and took away her gold and as they extracted every precious item from its cached hiding place, they stripped her even of her petticoats, and gagged and tied her to a chair. Later when they had assembled all their loot, they incised tiny gashes all over her body, applied salt to these cuts and left. In parting they told her that this was their gift for having her husband in the employ of the Portuguese. This story was just fresh in everyone's memory, and Aninha was twenty, nursing a rage against her husband and getting ready for a bath, when an alarm resounded through the village.

'The Ranes are coming!'

'*Rane eill go...*'

She did not hesitate. Leaving everything behind, she ran in her camisole in the direction of the vodd and plunged into it. She swam and swam, forgetting the pain and humiliation of the stitches to her head, forgiving her husband, missing her children and overcoming her depression. Nobody knew how it happened or why, but at the stroke of midnight, someone knocked on the door. Argentina had washed the dishes and was about to turn out the lamps in the dining room and retire for the night, when they heard a knock. It was the boatman. With his son and two helpers, he had carried the unconscious Aninha, wet as a fish, to her marital home. The boatman had found her near the river bank in a heap, shivering in her petticoat and had recognised her because he had ferried her as a bride. Given the crisis, she became the first woman to ford the temperamental river.

Support systems in a long and ongoing life

Victor Rangel-Ribeiro

Victor Rangel-Ribeiro began writing feverishly at a very early age. Eighty years later, geriatric specialists have confirmed what he has long suspected: the fever will never leave him. For this they spent years in medical college?

I remember school's out and we're on the

Mater Dei playground, a series of terraced steps cut into the hillside, each not more than ten yards wide. My teacher says ours is the best school in Goa but my brother Oscar says it's the best school in India and perhaps even in the whole Portuguese Empire. I'm surprised. 'Not in the world?' I ask. He thinks for a moment. 'Perhaps in the world,' he says. He should know. Oscar, whom I now see playing cricket two terraces down from where I'm standing, is thirteen. It's 1930. I'm five.

My friends and I used to play football here until yesterday, when our ball bounced down the slope all the way to the red mud road, and our teacher snatched it away; now we play tag with a ball that my mother stitched from an old sock stuffed with bits of cloth. It doesn't bounce at all, so teacher won't take it away.

In a few minutes Oscar will call out to me and we'll walk home. Our village is Porvorim, but we moved to Saligão a month ago, when Pai began teaching here. It would take us an hour to walk to our new home if we followed the road, but Oscar leads us through lanes and paths that branch off and wind between the houses. Pai goes home a different way. He leaves school after we do because he has things to do, but then he cuts quickly across the mown paddy fields and walks through the

Note: Although the author has had a life-long bond with all four of his siblings, in this memoir he focuses on ties with just one of them.

sugarcane plantations and gets home before us.

Today I see he is leaving early—that's him crossing the road below where I'm standing, and I know I must surprise him by going home with him instead of with Oscar and the others. I call out to Oscar that I'm going with Pai; he sees where I'm pointing and he nods. I hop down from terrace to terrace but my feet soon hurt and so at the next drop I slide. I slide again. At the road I turn to see Oscar watching me and I wave to show him I'm okay.

My father has long legs and I see him now farther away from me, so I call out excitedly, 'Pai! Pai!' and never mind the surprise. He does not hear me. I run as fast as I can and I'm gaining. But then I'm tired and he's in the fields on the winding path between the mowed-down paddy stalks and as long as he's in sight I can follow him and everything will be all right.

A man squats by the side of the path far away gathering hay and I hope my father will stop and talk to him as he usually stops to talk to people but he walks past the man and he gets smaller and smaller and the path takes him round the sugarcane field and then I can't see him at all. I have to pass the man who's cutting the hay and I start running again because I'm afraid of him and I'm crying. With tears flooding my eyes I can't see the path anymore and I stumble off it and fall. Stubble scrapes at my knees. Shocked, I stop crying.

There's a shadow beside me and strong hands pick me up and hold me high. It's the man I've been running from, but he's holding me gently and I look in his eyes and am no longer afraid. 'I'll take you home,' he says. 'Do you know where you live?'

Our lanes have no names and our houses have no numbers. How can I tell him where? I point beyond the sugarcane to where mango and coconut trees hide the rest of the village.

'You must be from the big house with the new family,' he says, 'I'll take you there.'

★ ★ ★

Dr. Miló Faria is a big doctor in the town of Mapusa, which lies north of Saligão, but my friends call him Dr. Phut-Phut. He comes riding into our village on his big old motorcycle, and that's the sound it makes as it comes down the lane that leads to our house. Dr. Phut-Phut comes to see me because once a month, when I'm playing marbles or seven tiles on the street, I'll get this urge to spit, and spit again and again, and my stomach will turn, and I'll have to run inside to the basin that's kept ready for me to vomit in. Nobody knows why this happens, though one neighbour lady says it must be the moon, and the lady who lives two houses further down says it's not the moon, it's tapeworm. She says the whole village has tapeworm and we should all be drinking chamomile tea and then everyone will be just fine. Another neighbour remembers seeing someone who has the evil eye pass by me just before I started spitting the very first time, months ago, and she says forget the tape-worm but send for the woman who gave me the evil eye so now she can take it away.

My mother sends instead for Dr. Miló and I'm glad. He spends a lot of time thumping on my chest and back and squeezing my stomach and he asks my mother what I like most to eat. After that each time he comes he calls out in a loud voice, right from the doorway: 'Give him salmon and green peas!' Just the thought of the pink salmon being taken out of its red can and put on my plate makes me feel better, never mind the peas. But when he says it especially loud, I know he is going to give me a needle, right where it hurts.

The woman who casts the evil eye now wants to cure me too. After she has the milky tea and the saucerful of roasted gram my grandmother gives her, she takes salt and chillies and stuff in her hand and passes it over my head and up and down muttering prayers and she throws it in the *chula* and it sounds like firecrackers. Sometimes she comes over just when I'm anxious to go out to play again. No matter which way I turn she's between me and the door. When I tell her not to bother with all the chillies and the prayers, because I'm not vomiting that day, she pinches both my cheeks and says to my mother, 'You see? It works!'

★ ★ ★

When Oscar is fourteen he gets into a fight with the village bully who is teasing me and my friends. Joachim is bigger but not as quick as Oscar and the two of them swirl around, Oscar punching as our cook has taught him to. Our cook says he was a boxing champion in Bombay, and Joachim knows that; so instead of punching he keeps trying to grab Oscar and push him off the road into the paddy field below. I lean down and pull out the largest handful of green paddy I can find and hit him on the shins with the stalks; Oscar yells at me to move away and when I won't he gets so mad he punches Joachim right in the mouth and breaks one of his teeth. I guess Oscar and I win this fight because Joachim runs home with blood on his shirt.

That same year the circus comes to Saligão and as I stand with my grandmother by the side of the road, she in her widow's weeds holding my hand, two older boys from our school come by on a bicycle, one sitting on the crossbar while the other pedals. We don't see them coming as we are busy looking at the little Chinese girl acrobats who are smaller even than me, and the camels and the elephants with richly dressed circus kids sitting proudly on their backs, and the clowns playing tricks on each other; the boys on the bike must be looking at all these things too because they ride straight into me and knock me down.

I'm lying half in the gutter with my legs on the road and, in a panic to get away, the boy who is pedaling finds he can't get the wheel over my calf so the two of them ride over my ankle instead. I cry out in pain and Granny shrieks a plague on the boys when she finds she cannot pick me up; a clown then hoists me on to his shoulders and carries me up our steps.

At the door to our house he stops and turns so I can see the lions and tigers go by in their cages. The tigers are bigger than the lions, but one of the lions turns to look at me and his mouth is open. His teeth are as long as my fingers; I close my eyes and turn my head away. But the clown says, 'Did you see those teeth, do you know the lion tamer sticks his head into that mouth twice a day, sometimes three times?' I know right away when I grow up I'll ride on a circus elephant, and be a clown perhaps, but a lion tamer never.

That evening my mother doesn't send for Dr. Phut-Phut because salmon and peas aren't going to help but instead sends our servant to fetch a bonesetter who lives in a far-off village. While we wait for him the sun sets and the jackals on the hill begin to howl. At once the circus lions roar and the jackals fall silent. Even Blackie our dog gets his tail between his legs. Pai says lions put their mouths to the ground when they roar so the sound then seems to come from everywhere and it confuses their prey. I ask him if they will roar the same way to confuse us if they come to our house and he says there's no way they can come because in a circus they are always kept in cages.

Still, after Pai leaves the room I call Oscar and tell him that if the lions come and he can't find me after they leave he should look for me on the canopy of my four-poster bed; we each have one. I ask him whether he thinks I will be safe up there. He stands by my bed and reaches up and his fingers are still short of the crossbars.

'You'll be safe,' he says.

'How about if it's a tiger?'

'Then, too.'

'Even if it stands on tippy-toes?'

'I was standing on tippy-toes,' Oscar says.

I tell him it will be okay for him to sleep next to me tonight if he likes and then if the lions come we can both fight them together or climb on to the canopy. He smiles and walks to the door and turns and makes a fist and flexes his muscle so it looks like there's a big mouse running up and down his upper arm. I know then that if a lion shows up Oscar will knock out its teeth all at once and not just one tooth the way he did Joachim's.

When the bonesetter comes, it is already ten o'clock at night. He is very old and has had to walk many miles over the hills to get here, but he has come anyway. He speaks to us in Konkani and calls me *babazinh*. He hasn't brought the thing Dr. Phut-Phut sticks in his ears, and he doesn't shout for salmon and peas; instead he grunts as he twists my leg this way and that, listening to clicks and howls of pain, until at last he has it right. He has brought a brown root and bamboo sticks tied in a red cloth, and he breaks the root into bits and grinds them into a paste with water. The messy stuff feels cold on my ankle and shin and the pain goes away.

While he is tying my leg in the bamboo sticks he asks my grandmother where she comes from. She says Anjuna; he knows people there, and asks for her family name. When she tells him 'Vaz', he exclaims, 'I know your family! Your uncle was a priest!'

She says, 'Why do you say it in that tone?'

He does not look at her and lowers his voice and says, 'When there's a priest in the family, the male line does not continue.'

He also finds out that she was the fifth child in a family of nine, the only girl. Again he clicks his tongue and says, 'That too is bad luck. Everybody knows that.'

For all his trouble he will accept a payment of only two rupees and a shot of cashew feni, and he drinks it quickly, smacking his lips, and is gone. Then I hear Granny repeating to my mother the things he has said and I ask what it means. My grandmother says, 'Not a thing.' But later I cannot sleep because Granny is saying a second Rosary very loudly, and when I ask my mother why, she says only that Granny is troubled, and wants me to get well.

The bonesetter has said I should stay in bed a month, but by the end of the first week I'm bored. The most I'm allowed to do is sit up. To tempt me to eat, my mother serves me special meals. My plate is brought to me each noon and night with a castle or fort in the centre, made some-times of mashed potatoes, sometimes of heaped-up rice. The surrounding moat she fills with gravy, or with *kalchi koddi*, which I love the most. Meat and vegetables come in a smaller plate on the side.

One day the vegetable is four pieces of boiled eggplant. I tell the cook the eggplant pieces look slippery and I know they'll taste like snails. I've never eaten snails but I know they must taste bad because Joachim the bully on his way home from school during the monsoon finds snails in flooded paddy fields by groping under water with his bare toes. Oscar says that when Joachim gets home he swallows them all, boiled.

I look at the snail-like eggplant and my stomach turns. 'I'll just eat the castle,' I say.

The cook calls Oscar. 'The castle belongs to the King of the Eggplants,' Oscar tells me. 'That's his army over there: four eggplant pieces, four regiments. How can you eat his castle, unless you first capture his army?'

What he says makes sense.

'With your knife, fork, teeth, and tongue,' Oscar adds hastily, when I make a quick grab to squish the eggplant pieces with my fingers.

At the end of the month, with the splints finally off, my right leg is white and shrivelled. I feel dizzy when I stand, and have to learn to walk all over again. The first time I leave the house it takes me long to go down the steps that lead to the road. I've hardly reached it when a strange dog comes loping along. Tail hanging low, tongue dripping foam and saliva, he staggers as he runs. I know the signs. 'Mad dog!' Joachim shouts. 'Mad dog! Run!' The village dogs too know the dog is sick, and have been driving him away in a pack, barking loudly, but not coming close— each time he turns and bares his teeth and snarls they back away.

The dog sees me and turns; I'm slow getting back into the garden. Oscar comes by then, and hurls stones as fast as he can find them; the dog turns and savagely bites each stone that hits him. We have reached the steps to our door and this time Oscar misses narrowly—the dog turns and hunts for the stone anyway. Oscar then swings his arm back and throws a stone past the dog as hard as he can, and when the dog chases after it, we make it all the way up to our front door.

My mother smacks my bottom twice for getting into danger and then hugs and kisses me.

When I'm seven, Oscar goes off to college in Bombay, a whole day's train journey away. It's June, and the monsoon rains are pouring down on us as we stand at the front gate and wave good-bye. All that rainwater on our faces makes it harder for him to see we're crying. Colem station is thirty miles from our house and he's riding there with his college-bound friends in a big old taxi; the luggage is piled so high on the roof it looks like they're in a bus. From Bombay he writes us cheerful letters that make me laugh and wish I could be at St. Xavier's, too.

War breaks out in Europe in 1939. The family moves to Bombay and Oscar is back with us. In mid-1941 I enrol in St. Xavier's and am thrilled to be walking down the long Gothic-arched corridors he has described so often and so well. As I press forward with dozens of my new classmates to our physics lab I see a burly, bushy-haired professor striding towards us. His eyes are pointed east and west but at the door to the lab he stops short, and points a finger at me. 'You there, Ribeiro!' he cries. 'Yes, you! I threw your brother out of my class eight years ago. Don't let the same thing happen to you!'

My companions laugh. I'm speechless. 'That's Professor Kothare,' one of them tells me. 'One of the best. And what a memory! Your brother must have been quite a fellow.' How true! But when I tell Oscar about the incident he laughs it off. 'My dear chap,' he says, 'I took his course eight years ago! Eight years! He has mistaken you and me for someone else. It's a clear case of mistaken nonentity.' Mistaken or not, it earns me some respect.

Not all my professors are as intimidating. One, Fred Mendonça, whose lectures I really like, lives in a world still peopled by John Donne, Edmund Spenser, Ben Jonson, Marlowe, and Shakespeare; he is so inspired by his subject that he stammers and stutters and repeats himself in his enthusiasm. But he embarrasses me in my third year by planting one foot on the bench a row ahead of where I sit, and directing his hour-long lecture at me. He does it, I know, because he mistakenly thinks I alone know whereof he speaks; but with his foot poised there on the bench, his pyjama leg shows beneath the trousers he is also wearing. He has dressed himself absentmindedly, and the class snickers.

The girls adore him, and take copious notes. To them, he sings a continuous refrain: 'Please don't hang upon my lips, don't hang upon my lips, don't hang upon my lips.' It seems that everything he says he repeats three times, sometimes for emphasis, sometimes to give note takers a chance to get things down on paper and get them right, sometimes just to gain time to marshal his thoughts.

At annual assemblies, which are part concert and part skits, I'm usually on stage, by demand, parodying one of his lectures. It's a popular item. I bend myself, as he does, into a question mark, and pace about the stage. 'Don't hang upon my lips!' I plead repeatedly, while the audience grows increasingly hysterical, and he himself is doubled up with laughter.

Even before I graduate, he and I are friends. I learn that in music his tastes are not Elizabethan but rooted in a later century; one Saturday after class he invites me over to his house, to listen to Beethoven. For reasons not quite clear to me he thinks my grasp of Beethoven's music is on a par with his grasp of Shakespeare. We take a tramcar to where he lives in Mazagon, and on that lumbering ride, above the wild clanging of the tram driver's bell and the grinding of the wheels and the shouts of the street vendors hawking their wares, he explains the problem he faces. 'It's the last quartets,' he says. 'I've read that they're great music and I sense that they're great, but I do not understand them, try as I might I do not understand them, I do not understand them at all.' The man is distraught. I try to tell him that I don't understand them either; not many people do.

'Explain them to me,' he still insists. I wish I could find some way to tell him not to hang upon my lips. He has an old-fashioned wind-up phonograph with a horn, and he places one RCA Victor 78 rpm on the turntable at a time, flipping it over when the side is done. We sit there by the hour, he getting up every four or five minutes to change a disc or wind up the ancient instrument. He uses Japanese bamboo needles instead of steel because bamboo does not wear out the grooves as much, but some of the 78s are warped, and when he puts these on the turntable the sound box seems to be riding an endless succession of waves.

He plays recordings by the Busch Quartet, and by the Budapest; both leave him excited and baffled. He still asks, plaintively, 'What does it mean?' I tell him Beethoven cannot be explained, not the way one can explain Othello, or Hamlet; we just have to listen until the music becomes part of us. Then it dawns on me that he needs me there, at least until that happens, until Beethoven becomes a part of him. He has brought a brave new world of literature into my life; I must do the same for him in music. So the Saturday sessions continue, even after I graduate.

★ ★ ★

By mid-1942 the Japanese are sweeping through Burma on their way to India; Oscar volunteers into the army. He is given a commission and when he comes home on furlough we see he has grown a moustache and is affecting a stiff upper lip and the trace of a British accent. I particularly like the way he carries his swagger stick—the right forearm bent at right angles, one end of the stick in the palm of his hand, the other tucked into his armpit.

The day after he leaves I find myself saying 'What ho!' and 'old chap,' and 'pip-pip!' instead of cheerio; my friends find out why and look at me in awe. In 1945 the Japanese surrender. Though two atom bombs had much to do with it, Oscar too must have played a part.

He comes home then, but just as we think he's home for good, he joins an international news agency. My mother says he's doing it to further his career, but I think it's because two aunts have been conspiring to get him married, and he has joined this foreign outfit to escape their plotting; it's like joining the French Foreign Legion, only instead of being sent off to the Sahara he gets sent to Paris.

In 1948 he writes that he'll be passing through Bombay en route to Rangoon, to cover the Catholic Karen tribesmen's rebellion against their Buddhist masters. Oscar says he won't be able to see us because they are only making a refuelling stop in Bombay, but I find out that the plane will be there two hours, and take a train and then a taxi to Juhu aerodrome. Unfortunately, Oscar's plane has landed at the newly opened Santa Cruz airport. The taxi has left and I don't have enough money on me anyway, so I run the five miles between the two. To psyche myself I picture the hostess already standing by the boarding gate; I hear the crowds roaring out my name, egging me on. People I pass point the way. At last I'm racing in a straight line and the finish is in sight. My stride quickens.

At the Air France desk I have Oscar paged and we talk across a barrier and he sees me flushed and drenched in sweat. 'I had a feeling you'd come,' he says. 'I looked for you as soon as we got off the plane, and when I didn't see you, I thought, ah, well. But even then something told me you'd come.'

We talk sibling talk. His flight is called, with half our thoughts unsaid. No matter; in one giant hug he says it all, for both of us.

I meet him next five years later when I'm in Calcutta as Sunday editor with the *Times of India* and he is passing through on another assignment. We lunch in style at the Grand Hotel's Palm Court, with a piano trio playing Viennese waltzes as well as the latest popular hits—'In the Mood', 'Chattanooga Choo-Choo', 'Gal in Kalamazoo'. After lunch we take in an Arthur Rank comedy about a professor running amok in the English countryside, and we laugh hysterically, but the very serious Bengali audience shushes us repeatedly because they want to savour every last misplaced quotation from Shakespeare.

Fifty years have elapsed since that uproarious afternoon. Oscar and I each have married; he lives in Europe, I in the United States; we both have raised families, become grandparents, and kept in close touch over the years, though now that I'm in my mid-eighties and he's edged past ninety it is not easy. Bad eyesight, broken bones, that sort of thing. He writes me funny letters; I'd much rather use the telephone. He uses it more often.

When the phone rings and our bedroom is pitch dark and the clock radio dial tells me it's not yet five in the morning, I know it's him. His first words invariably are, 'I didn't wake you up, did I?' and just as often I deny that he did, because it's wonderful to hear his voice.

A few years ago, when he had flown in for my fourth grand-child's christening, I said to him that despite all the celebrating, getting old is depressing business. And he said, 'Is it depressing business in general, or is it depressing some particular business? You hear undertakers complaining? Pharmacists? Or those who are getting rich selling cemetery plots, well ahead of time?'

I said, 'I mean that getting old is depressing me, and you are depressing me even further.' 'You'll depress yourself right into a depression in the ground,' he said. 'Look at me! Do I look depressed?'

I looked at him - he was in excellent shape, and that was the most depressing sight of all. Just months earlier, years after he had retired from the ILO, one of his former secretaries had met him and gushed, 'Cher M'sieur Ribeiro, you haven't changed one bit!' to which Oscar had replied, 'My dear child, once you've reached perfection, why bother to change?' Which flustered her so much that he changed it to, 'I mean, once one has become fossilized, it is impossible to change.' Even today, though he is living in an assisted living facility, he has the air of someone

already planning to celebrate his one-hundredth birthday by swimming across Lake Geneva on his back, towing one hundred kayaks by
a rope clenched between his teeth. The very thought of it makes my
dentures ache.

'It's our support system,' I tell him. 'It's eroding. You and I came
into this world with a strong supportive network: mother, midwife, grandmother, sisters, servants, and a father pacing the parlour while chewing
on a cigar. As we grew up, there were others who were also quite supportive, that we've lost track of. It's a shame, a downright shame.'

'Doctors with syringes,' he says. 'Dentists with drills—'

'I miss our teachers the most,' I say. 'One in high school, he had a
walrus moustache. Baptista. Then, in college, those brilliant professors
who thought the world of us, forecasting great things. Gone, every last
one of them.'

I see that I've finally touched him. He remains silent awhile, lips
quivering, battling a profound emotion. 'Don't take it to heart,' he says
at last. 'Sometimes we focus too much on ourselves; look instead on the
bright side of things. Think again of the professors, who as you say pro-
jected such wonderful futures for each of us. To them, we were also a
support system, and it's a good thing they're gone. Not only are they
happy in heaven, but had they lived on and seen us now, think how
disappointed they would have been!'

'And now that I've got you smiling,' he says, nodding at the babble
of happy voices coming from the next room, where guests have gathered
around my little grandson's crib. 'You remember the old bonesetter's pre-
diction, which upset our mother and our grand-mother so much. He
said our line would end. Well, he too was wrong,' Oscar says. 'Our line
continues.'